Paneling &
Wallcoverings

By Richard V. Nunn

ISBN: 0-8487-0442-8
Library of Congress Catalog Card Number: 76-9275

Manufactured in the United States of America

First Printing 1976

Paneling & Wallcoverings

Editor: Karen Phillips
Cover Photograph: The Masonite Corporation
Photography: Louis Joyner, Bob Lancaster

Contents

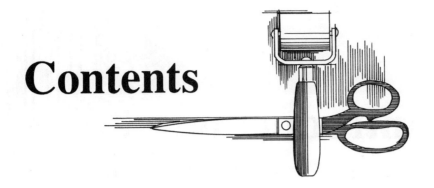

Introduction

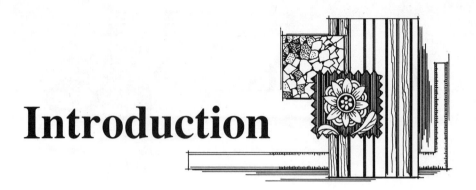

Even if you own a brand new home, chances are that the walls in the house are not plumb (vertically level) or perfectly smooth and flat.

Since this imperfect wall condition exists in most homes, *Paneling & Wallcoverings* can be of great service when you install paneling, hang wallpaper, or cover any wall with one of the specialty wallcoverings.

This book shows and tells you how to fit wallcoverings to almost any kind of wall surface, saving plenty of time. Some of the techniques are easy; others are more complicated. But, certainly, the more complicated techniques are not beyond the skills of most home handymen.

Patience, concern for detail, and neatness are the keys to smart-looking results when you hang wallpaper, panel a room, or put up mirror tile. Take the time to prepare the walls properly and to fit the material to the walls, and you will have a professional job that you will be proud to show your friends.

You are in luck when it comes to wallcovering materials. Through new technology, wallcovering manufacturers offer a wide range of products—from fancy, embossed, vinyl-coated wallpapers and foil and flocked papers to handsome wooden wall paneling to simulated brick and stone to ceramic tile.

One chapter in the book contains photographs of rooms utilizing various wall materials; the intent is to give you an idea of what is available and how the material may look in your home. We hope this chapter will inspire you to shop in wallcovering stores to find the right product for a special room in your home.

The other chapters explain how to install various wallcovering materials. We think that you will find these methods fairly easy to follow and that you will be able to add your own expertise to a project as it progresses.

Be sure to ask many questions when you purchase wallcoverings. Some products have specific manufacturers' recommendations as to the proper installation of the product. This is especially true with some of the new flocked and foil papers. Also, ask for any manufacturers' literature available; this instructional material can be most helpful.

Finally, and perhaps best of all, we think you will gain a lot of personal satisfaction in putting up one or more of the new wallcoverings yourself—not to mention the money you can save.

The Wonderful World of Wallcoverings

There are so many types, colors, and textures of wallcoverings today that it will take you plenty of time to make a choice. But this is the fun of it—making your home just what you want it to be.

Before you start a project, you should shop all the wallcovering outlets in your area. You will find most of them listed in your telephone book. Do not overlook home center stores, building material outlets, and the big catalog stores. Many of these retailers have a wide selection in wallcoverings.

You should thumb through the various consumer magazines and special issues of magazines that may be found on most newstands. Also, pick up all the wallcovering literature you can find from manufacturers.

When selecting wallcoverings, there are no hard and fast rules to follow. Your home should be a part of you and reflect your life-style.

Installing a wallcovering is one of the quickest ways to change the appearance of your home. You can make a room appear smaller or larger with certain wallcoverings. You may also lower or raise a ceiling with certain color, pattern, and texture. There are some other considerations:

- Use your imagination with the various materials available. For example, you don't have to panel an entire room. An accent wall may be just enough to set off a sofa or a conversation area, emphasize the frame on a favorite picture, or enhance a fireplace wall.
- Try to use a variety of wallcoverings. However, make sure the colors in your home are compatible.
- Blend the wallcovering with the other items in the room, such as the carpeting, window shades, shutters, paintings, furniture, room dividers, fireplaces, bookshelves, and storage cabinets.
- Look for wallcoverings with hidden assets: surfaces that are easy to clean; surfaces that will withstand abuse from children; strippable wallcoverings that can be removed easily; and materials that you can easily install yourself.
- Although you will need to stay within your decorating budget, don't be afraid to buy a quality product.

Color photographs from books, magazines, and manufacturers' literature can be very beneficial when you shop for wallcoverings. Take along all the ideas you can. Also, if you have color swatches of fabric that you want to coordinate with a wallcovering, be sure to include the swatches in your shopping portfolio. When you provide a sales person with a picture or a paint chip, he can help you make a better selection.

In this chapter, we have provided you with a potpourri of photographs of wallcoverings. It would be impossible for us to show you every wallcovering pattern or design available. However, these photographs may give you an idea or two that will be helpful in selecting a wallcovering.

Wallcoverings for special effects

Simulated brick panels were used to create this room divider. The cabinet, which is set in the recessed walls of the fireplacelike divider, provides plenty of storage and serving space. Note how the beams and the paneling as well as the furnishings in the adjoining room carry out the "country kitchen" theme of the room.

These hardboard panels not only serve as a wallcovering, but as the covering for a handy storage area. The hardboard material is also used to face the window seat, which stores games and other items. The informality of the wall paneling is carried out further in the red, white, and blue patchwork design in the vinyl-asbestos tile. Also, the patchwork design is carried out in the drapery fabric. The total cost for the wall paneling, flooring, and drapery fabric in this 12- by 16-foot room was under $200.

Foil wallcovering brightens this dining room and enlarges it through a muted reflection. The wainscotting helps give the foil balance and adds interest to the room.

Wallcoverings with an open print provide a "see through" look. They are especially attractive in small rooms, such as this breakfast area. The French doors were painted white to pick up the flower colors in the wallcovering; the furnishings were also chosen to coordinate with the colors in the wallcovering.

A bright cane-patterned wallcovering perks up this sunroom. The pedestal is covered with the same cane pattern to give more depth to the room. The furnishings complement the wall-covering—even down to the live green plants. Each wallcovering panel is spaced about 6 inches apart, and the wall between is painted white to give the room a vertical appearance.

Matching fabric covers this single wall panel to carry out the theme in a child's room. The walls were painted an accent color from the fabric. The fabric could have been pasted directly to the wall. But, by mounting the fabric on a piece of ¾-inch plywood, the wallcovering gives the wall depth. The carpeted platform with a mattress on it is augmented by sleeping bags for overnight guests.

Knotty pine tongue-and-groove boards are refinished with a walnut stain varnish in this study. Somewhat the same effect could be created with random-grooved, walnut plywood paneling. The lighter-colored furnishings complement the wall.

Wainscotting around the bottom half of a wall doesn't have to be wood; it can be a foil, burlap, grass cloth, or any other flexible wallcovering. The remaining part of the wall can be covered with paint, paneling, cork, or mirror tile. The white furnishings complement the subtle, dark colors of the wallcoverings. Even the picture frames pick up the metallic colors in the foil wainscotting.

A smart graphic design combines metallic foil and paint. The colors in the room add to the design and provide an ultramodern look. To produce this effect, you must carefully lay out the design on the wall. Apply the paint first; then install the foil (you can use contact paper).

Random-grooved plywood paneling was used to give this room more height to highlight the open-beamed ceiling. The paneling goes up to the gables on the ends of the room. The color of carpeting picks up the wall colors; the furnishings pick up the color of the beams and wall hangings.

Wallcovering Tools

The tools and materials that you will need for a wallcovering project depend on the type of wallcovering. You will not have to spend a lot of money on equipment; however, we suggest that you purchase quality tools, because they will help you do a better job.

Brushes, rollers, razor knives, and scrapers are inexpensive. Conversely, hammers and levels are more expensive. However, if you buy a quality hammer or level, you will be able to use this equipment for a lifetime on many other home repair and improvement projects. Consider it an investment.

This chapter includes different wallcovering projects and the tools and materials that are needed for each project.

Wall paneling

There are two techniques used to install wall paneling: adhesive applied directly to the wall surface and furring strips fastened to the studs with nails. If the walls are fairly smooth and in good condition, we recommend the adhesive method. If the walls are bellied out or sunken you should use furring strips; the strips will level the walls. Both techniques are explained in the chapter on wall paneling installation.

To install paneling with adhesive, you will need these supplies:
- 13-ounce claw hammer
- Fine-tooth saw, 10½ points (or teeth) per inch
- Coping saw
- Brace and ½-inch bit
- Keyhole saw

- Panel adhesive
- Caulking gun, cartridge type
- Colored paneling nails
- Plumb bob and chalk line
- 2 pounds of 6d (penny) finishing nails—for the average-size room
- 1 spray can of flat, black enamel
- Wiping rags
- 2 putty sticks (color depends on color of panels)
- 1-inch wood chisel

To install paneling with furring strips, you will need the following:
- 13-ounce claw hammer
- Fine-tooth saw, 10½ points (or teeth) per inch
- Coping saw
- Brace and ½-inch bit
- Keyhole saw
- 1-inch wooden chisel
- Level
- Carpenter's square
- Plumb bob and chalk line
- Colored paneling nails depending on color of panels
- 5 pounds of 6d (penny) finishing nails—for the average-size room
- 1 spray can of flat, black enamel
- Wiping rags
- 2 putty sticks (color depends on color of panels)

If you are going to put paneling over a masonry surface, you will need additional equipment.
- Star drill for masonry anchors (You can also use a masonry drill bit in a portable electric drill).
- Masonry anchors

Wallpaper

To hang wallpaper, you will need these tools and supplies:

- Pasting table—You can put two card tables together and top the tables with a sheet of ¼-inch tempered hardboard. The table should be at least 6 feet long. You may be able to rent a pasting table from a rental outlet.
- Two buckets—One bucket is for paste; the other bucket is for clear water.
- Water tray—if the paper is prepasted
- 1 paste brush—If you prefer, you may use a paint roller and roller tray.
- Tape measure
- Razor knife with a package of extra blades
- Straightedge, 8 feet long—We recommend a lightweight aluminum angle.
- Plumb bob and chalk line
- 12-inch wide smoothing brush
- Seam roller
- Long-bladed shears
- 6-foot stepladder (if you paper ceilings) or sturdy stool
- Drop cloths
- Sponge
- Scraper or putty knife

Mirror tile

To install mirror tile, you will need these supplies:

- Glass cutter
- Plumb bob and chalk line
- Builder's panel adhesive and caulking gun (if adhesive pads are not furnished with the tile)
- Tape measure
- 12-inch ruler or yardstick
- 12-inch length of ½-inch dowel rod

Cork tile

To install cork tile, you will need these supplies:

- Plumb bob and chalk line
- Level
- Razor knife and package of extra blades
- Notched adhesive spreader and adhesive (if the tiles are not prepasted)

Ceramic tile

To install ceramic tile, you will need these supplies:

- Level
- Plumb bob and chalk line
- Glass cutter
- Pliers
- Notched adhesive spreader
- Adhesive
- Putty knife or scraper
- Sponge
- Water bucket

Simulated brick and stone (panel type)

To install simulated brick and stone, you will need these supplies:

- Plumb bob and chalk line
- Level
- Hammer
- 2 pounds of 6d (penny box nails or gypsum board nails)
- Hacksaw
- Caulking gun (cartridge type)—if the joints are not pregrouted

Simulated brick and stone (individual type)

- Plumb bob and chalk line
- Level
- Notched adhesive spreader
- Hacksaw
- Coarse abrasive and sanding block

Wall preparation tools

Wall surfaces usually have to be repaired before wallcoverings can be applied; holes and dents must be patched. An exception is wall paneling; the panels will cover the imperfections.

The tools for this job include:

- Hammer
- Crosscut saw
- Wide wall scraper
- Level
- Coarse-grit and medium-grit sandpaper and sanding block
- 1-inch wide chisel
- Tuck-pointing trowel (if you work with concrete block or brick)
- Water bucket

Below is an explanation of why we have recommended certain tools.

Hammer. A 13-ounce hammer is easier for the home handyman to use than a 16-ounce hammer. We recommend a hammer with a rubber or synthetic covering over the handle—especially if you will be installing paneling. The covering protects the paneling when you are nailing on trim and moldings; you will probably hit the paneling with the handle when you are pounding in tight quarters.

Level. Buy a long level—3-bubble—since you get a more accurate reading than with a short level. This level will give you the vertical level as well as the horizontal level; you may also use the level as a straightedge.

Pasting table. Most rental outlets have paste tables available for about $10 per day (average). You can also put together two card tables and top them with a sheet of plywood or hardboard (¾-inch plywood costs about $25; hardboard costs about $8) for a smooth pasting surface. If you use plywood, give the surface a coat of shellac to protect it from the moisture of the paste.

Crosscut saw. We recommend that you use a crosscut saw with 10½ teeth per inch for sawing paneling; this configuration will give you a smoother cut. When working with a power saw, you should use a fine combination blade or a crosscut blade to saw paneling. Always saw paneling with the good side up, and support the panel so that the saw doesn't bind. If you use a power saw to cut the panels, cut with the best side of the panel down.

If you need to plane the panels, always plane from the ends toward the middle; this will prevent splitting the corners and edges. If you have to sand the panel, use a medium-grit abrasive and go easy; you can quickly cut through the veneer.

Screwdrivers. There are two types of screwdrivers: Phillips head and standard blade. You will need one or the other—or perhaps both—to remove plates from wall switches, outlets, and heating and cooling registers.

Putty knives and scrapers. You have a choice of stiff-bladed or flexible-bladed knives and scrapers. We recommend the stiff type; after a little practice, it is easier to use.

Paste brush. We recommend that you use an 8-inch brush with 4-inch bristles. You can also use a paint roller to apply the paste to the back of wallpaper; however, we prefer the brush.

Buckets. We recommend that you buy two 2½-gallon galvanized buckets. You need one bucket for paste and one bucket for clear water for cleanup. You can also use plastic buckets, but buy the sturdy ones.

Straightedge. You must have a straightedge to hang any of the flexible wallcoverings, but a professional straightedge is expensive. We recommend a 10-foot length of ¾-inch aluminum angle. The angle will cost about $6; it is lightweight and has a true straight edge.

Seam roller. There are many types of seam rollers. Flat rollers are used for smoothing large areas around the seam of the wallcovering; beveled rollers are used for pressing down the seam. You can buy plastic and wooden rollers. If you are hanging a heavy vinyl wallcovering, buy a steel seam roller.

Cutting wheel. This tool has a round, steel wheel with a razor-sharp edge. It may have teeth. You use the cutting wheel to trim around windows, doors, and baseboards. This tool is not readily available. If you cannot find a cutting wheel, a razor knife is a good substitute.

Plumb bob. You need this tool to establish a true vertical line. You also need a length of chalk line and chalk. You can establish the vertical line with a level, but a plumb bob is easier to use.

Smoothing brush. Buy a 12-inch brush to sweep out air bubbles trapped under wallpaper. You can use a squeegee for this, but we recommend the brush; it is easier to handle.

Sponge. Any type of sponge can be used on wallcoverings. You need the sponge to wipe away excess paste on the face of the wallcovering.

Scissors. For trimming around doors, windows, and electrical outlets, we recommend 12-inch shears. If you will be hanging fabrics or heavy vinyl papers, scissors with shorter blades work better.

How to Estimate Wallcovering Needs

Estimating your material needs is an important part of the wallcovering project. Measure accurately before you purchase any materials. If you overestimate your requirements, the leftover materials may not be able to be returned to the store. This, of course, can make your project more expensive.

On the other hand, underestimating your material needs can be a problem, too. Some materials are made in certain quantities, and the manufacturer may be out of the pattern you want when you reorder it. Also, the patterns and colors of some materials vary.

If you go about it in a systematic way, estimating the amount of wallcovering you need for a room is not difficult. In this chapter, we include several estimating charts to help you figure material; we also include several tips.

Wall paneling

Most wall paneling is sold in 4- by 8-foot sheets. You can also buy 4- by 9- and 4- by 10-foot sheets; these usually have to be ordered.

There are three types of wall paneling: solid wood, plywood, and hardboard. Solid wood paneling is, of course, expensive. Plywood and hardboard are usually moderate in cost, although walnut and cherry panels can be fairly expensive.

Wall paneling varies in thickness from ⅛ inch to ¾ inch. The ⅛-inch material is satisfactory, but it must be backed by a solid wall such as lath and plaster or gypsum wallboard. If your project involves fastening panels over bare studs, the panels should be at least ¼ inch thick.

To measure a room for paneling, determine the perimeter of the room. The perimeter is the total of the widths of each wall in the room. For example, one wall may be 8 feet wide, another wall 10 feet wide, the third wall 7 feet wide, and the fourth wall 8 feet wide. The perimeter of the room is 33 feet. If the perimeter of your room falls between the figures given on the conversion chart below, go to the next higher number.

Conversion Chart for Wall Paneling

Room Perimeter in feet	Number of Panels Needed
20	5
24	6
28	7
32	8
60	15
64	16
68	17
72	18
92	23

Moldings and trim

Prefinished moldings are usually sold in 7-foot lengths. Ready-to-finish moldings can vary in length—from 8 feet to 16 feet. The moldings you will be most concerned with are base molding, inside corner molding or cove molding, outside corner molding, and shoe molding or crown molding.

Molding patterns are varied, and it would be impossible to list them all. For paneling projects, use the moldings mentioned above—or one of the variations of these. If you have a specific problem, your building materials retailer will help you make a selection. Moldings are usually sold by the linear foot; the configuration of the molding will determine its price. For example, crown molding will cost more than quarter-round molding.

Flexible wallcovering

Although no one has probably ever counted them, there must be a thousand different wallpaper patterns. Your biggest problem will be in making a selection.

A single roll of wallpaper covers 30 square feet—no matter how wide the roll is. A single roll of wallpaper contains 35 square feet. However, you should count on getting 30 square feet out of each roll since you have to allow for waste as you trim and match the wallcovering.

The technique for measuring a room to determine the amount of flexible wallcovering you will need is similar to that of wall paneling. Follow these steps:

1. Determine the height of each wall from the baseboard to the ceiling.
2. Measure the distance around the room at the baseboard.
3. Determine the amount of material you need from the chart.

Estimating Chart for Flexible Wallcovering

Distance Around Room (feet)*	*Ceiling Height			Yards for Border	*Rolls for Ceiling
	8 feet	9 feet	10 feet		
28	8	8	10	11	2
30	8	8	10	11	2
32	8	10	10	12	2
34	10	10	12	13	4
36	10	10	12	13	4
38	10	12	12	14	4
40	10	12	14	15	4
42	12	12	14	15	4
44	12	12	14	16	4
46	12	14	14	17	6
48	14	14	16	17	6
50	14	14	16	18	6
52	14	14	16	19	6
54	14	16	18	19	6
56	14	16	18	20	8
58	16	16	18	21	8
60	16	18	20	21	8
62	16	18	20	22	8
64	16	18	20	23	8
66	18	20	20	23	10
68	18	20	22	24	10
70	18	20	22	25	10
72	18	20	22	25	12
74	20	22	22	26	12
76	20	22	24	27	12
78	20	22	24	27	14
80	20	22	26	28	14
82	22	24	26	30	14
84	22	24	26	30	16
86	22	24	26	30	16
88	24	26	28	31	16
90	24	26	28	32	18

*This chart is figured on single rolls for the wall and the ceiling area. Deduct one roll for every three windows and one roll for every two doors.

Adhesives

Use one pound of wheat paste for six to eight rolls of wallcovering. If you have a mildew problem, buy paste with a mildew-resistant additive. You should always use a mildew-resistant adhesive with coated wallcoverings.

same—as standard field tile. To estimate how many of these tiles you will need, divide the length of the wall by 5 inches. In the case of 6-inch long edging, divide the length of the wall by 6 inches. For example, if the wall is 12 feet (144 inches) wide, you will need 24 pieces of edging to cap off

Adhesive Chart

Type of Wallcovering	Adhesive to Use
Standard wallpaper	Wheat paste or stainless paste
Strippable wallpaper	Liquid strippable paste or wheat paste
Foils	Vinyl adhesive
Backed burlap	Vinyl adhesive
Unbacked burlap	Wheat paste or stainless paste
Vinyl wallcoverings	Vinyl adhesive
Cork with backing	Vinyl adhesive
Fabrics (including silk)	Stainless paste
Hand prints, borders, flocked paper, murals	Vinyl adhesive

Note: If you overlap one strip of vinyl wallcovering with another strip of vinyl wallcovering, you will have to use vinyl-to-vinyl adhesive. Vinyl wallpapers are water resistant; therefore, regular adhesive will not stick the paper to the wall properly.

If you are hanging vinyl wallcovering, one gallon of vinyl adhesive is adequate to hang two to four rolls of wallcovering.

You should check the manufacturer's recommendations on any adhesive you purchase. Some wallcoverings will require more adhesive than others.

Estimating ceramic tile

Ceramic tile (standard field tile) is generally manufactured in 4¼- by 4¼-inch units. You can buy larger-size tiles, but these units are usually used for accents and are installed along with the basic-size tile.

To estimate how much tile you will need, multiply the length and the height of the area to be covered. Multiply this figure by two. If the room has a door or window, subtract the number of tiles that would be required to cover it. Then add two dozen tiles to the total figure. This extra tile will take care of any breakage during installation.

Besides standard field tile, you will also need edging caps, base tiles, and cove base corners. An edging cap usually measures 6 inches long by 2 inches wide. The other pieces measure the same—or about the

the field tile. (See estimating chart.)

You will need one gallon of ceramic tile adhesive for every fifty square feet of wall area.

You will need one pound of ceramic tile grout for every eighteen square feet of wall area.

Ceramic Tile Estimating Chart

Wall Measurement in Square Feet	Tile Needed
5	15
6	17
7	20
8	23
9	26
10	29
11	32
12	34
13	37
14	40
15	43

Specialty wallcoverings

This category includes cork tile, mirror tile, and simulated brick and stone. These wallcoverings are usually sold by the package. For example, cork tile, which measures 12 by 12 inches, is usually packed with 4 pieces or 4 square feet to a package. To determine the amount of material you will need to cover a wall, find the dimensions of the wall area.

If you use an adhesive to install cork, mirror, or brick and stone, refer to the manufacturer's recommendations on the package for the amount of adhesive necessary. The amount of adhesive you use may depend on the wall surface.

Many specialty wallcoverings come with the adhesive on the product. You peel off a paper backing and stick the product in position.

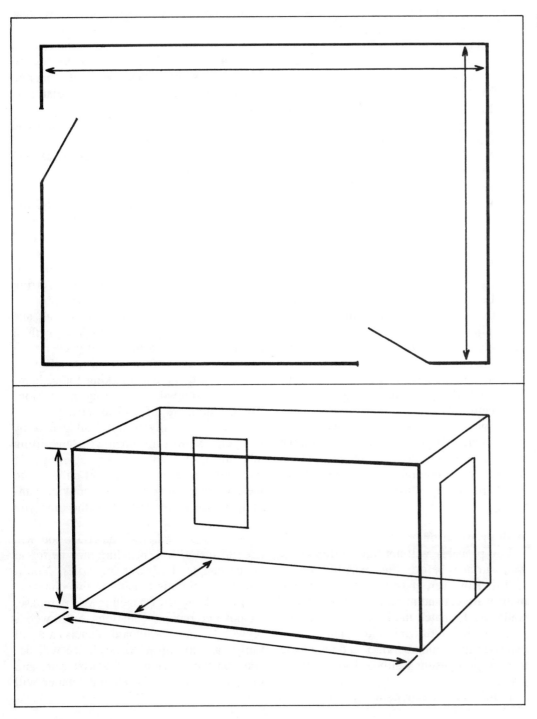

To find the perimeter of a room, figure the total of the widths (W) and the lengths (L) of the room.

To determine the amount of wallpaper you will need, measure the height (H) of the wall from the baseboard to the ceiling. Then measure the perimeter (L-length and W-width). Use the estimating chart to determine the amount of material you will need based on your measurements.

How to Install Wall Paneling

Of all the wallcoverings, wall paneling is probably the easiest to install. The material comes in big sheets (4- by 8-, 4- by 9-, and 4- by 10-feet) that can cover a large area fast.

Before you start actual installation:

1. Remove the furniture from the room that you will panel. If this is impossible, try to stack the furniture in the center of the room. You need the space next to the walls to fit the panels.
2. Remove all of the molding and trim in the room. Also, remove electrical switch and outlet covers and the heating/cooling registers.
3. Loosely stack the panels around the room, leaning them against the wall. Let the panels sit for at least 2 days (3 to 4 days is better) so that they can adjust to the humidity in the room. If the wood is damp when you install the panels, they may shrink from the heat in the room. Then you will have open joints where the panels fit together.

Although it is not necessary, we usually recommend that you stack and position the panels around the room so that you can get the best color and grain effect. This takes a lot of lifting and shifting, but it is worthwhile.

Wall preparation

You probably will not have to repair the wall surface before the paneling is installed. However, if you have a huge hole in the wall, cut and insert a piece of gypsum wallboard to match the hole. Then nail the patch to the studs and/or top and bottom plates (framing members). You do not have to tape the gypsum wallboard joints at the patch.

If the walls are fairly smooth, sound, and plumb (vertically level), we suggest that you install the panels with adhesive.

If the walls have irregular surfaces, you will have to install the panels over furring strips. Masonry walls made of concrete block and brick may have irregular surfaces.

If the irregular wall is made of lath and plaster or gypsum wallboard, you will still have to use furring strips to attach the paneling. This will assure a smooth paneling job.

When paneling directly over studs, use lengths of 2 by 4s at the top and bottom of the panels. The 2 by 4s give additional support to the panels, which have to be attached to the furring or studs on all four sides of the panel. Adhesive and furring techniques are shown in this chapter.

Wall paneling is a rugged material, and most of it has been prefinished with a tough, plasticlike top coat. However, you should try not to scratch the panels with nails, measuring and marking tools, hammers, and screwdrivers during installation. These marks are difficult to repair.

You can usually install wall panels by yourself. However, when you are fitting and cutting, you may need a helper to hold the panels so that you can get an accurate measurement. A professional-looking paneling job depends greatly on the time you spend with detail.

The list of tools and materials you will need to install wall paneling may be found in the chapter *Wallcovering Tools.* You'll also find estimating charts in this chapter.

As to the type of paneling you purchase, we have no recommendations. Solid wood, plywood, and hardboard panels are all fairly easy to apply. Your choice will depend on the panel style that you want and the cost. A building material retailer will help you.

How to remove obstructions from walls

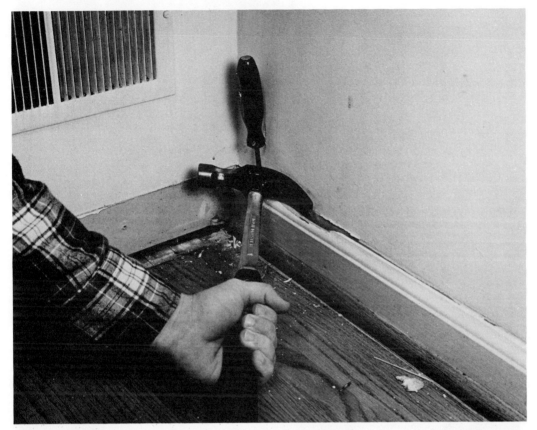

Baseboard, window and door casing, chair rail, crown molding, and other trim must be removed from the wall surfaces before the paneling can be installed. This is much easier than trying to cut and fit the panels around the molding. Since the existing molding probably won't match the paneling, you don't have to worry about splitting the molding when you remove it. Use a hammer and an old chisel or a screwdriver to pry off the moldings. Then, with the hammer, pull out all nails that protrude from the molding. Otherwise, you run the risk of stepping on a nail in the molding and hurting yourself. Also, molding without nails is easier to stack and carry to the trash—or burn as kindling in your fireplace.

Wall-mounted heating and cooling registers are usually fastened to the wall with screws. Simply back out the screws and remove the register. You should mark the position of each register in the room so that the register may be installed over the duct from which it was removed. Electrical switch and outlet plates are also held in position with screws. Remove the screws and the plates, marking them for position. As you work, try to sweep up any chunks of gypsum wallboard, plaster, and sawdust; otherwise these can be tracked all over your home.

Protruding windowsills can cause problems when you fit the panels. An easy solution is to saw off the projection so that the sill is flush with the window stop or built-in casing of the window. Smooth the cut with a medium-grit abrasive before the window is refinished or the adjoining panel is set in position.

If you prefer to trim the protruding windowsill, you can notch it with a chisel so that the panel may be slipped behind the sill. Be careful when you make the cut. Hard blows with a hammer can split the entire sill or one end of it. The apron (trim piece under the sill) on windows should be removed. This molding is replaced with molding that matches the paneling.

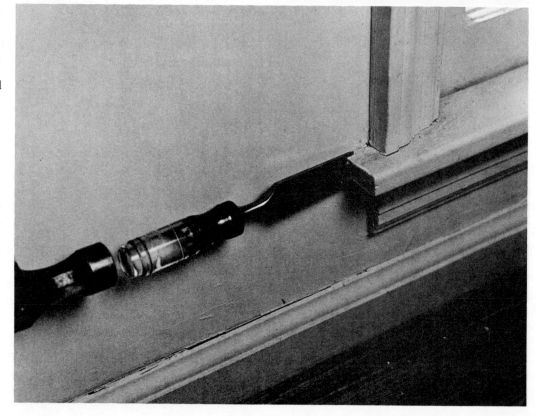

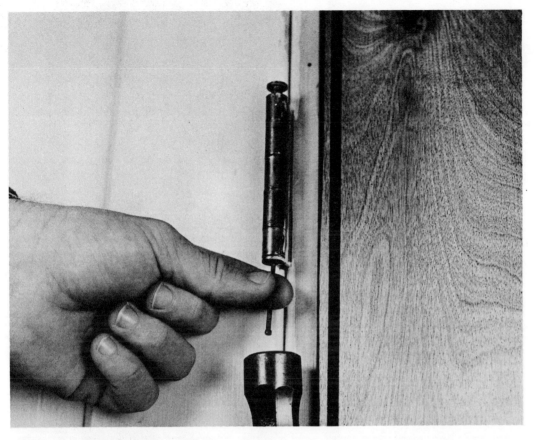

Remove doors to the room. It is easier to fit the paneling around the opening with the doors off the hinges. To remove the hinge pin, insert a nail in the hole at the bottom of the hinge, as shown, and tap out the pin with a hammer. If you can't find a hole at the bottom of the hinge, wedge a piece of scrap wood between the hinge leaf and the top of the pin, and tap the pin up and out with a hammer.

If the wall is smooth and even, paneling may be put over concrete block with adhesive. If gobs of mortar project from the wall, remove the mortar with an abrasive brick that you can buy at a building material outlet. If the wall is uneven, you will have to install furring strips. First, you need to measure the wall for the furring strips. The strips are 1 by 3s; space them 16 inches apart horizontally and 48 inches apart vertically. Holes for the masonry anchors may be punched in the wall with a star drill. We recommend that you wear safety glasses when you use this drill. To use a star drill, twist it into the wall as you strike the drill with a hammer. Use a sledgehammer if you have one.

Tap the plastic, fiber, or lead masonry anchors into the holes you drilled. The anchors should be spaced about every 2 feet, and they should be flush with the wall surface. To locate the fastening points on the furring strips, insert small nails in the anchors. Position the furring over the nails, level the furring, and tap the furring with a hammer. You'll need a helper for this. The nails will mark the drill points. Drill pilot holes for the screws at these points; then, run the screws through the furring into the anchors.

The fastest way to drill holes for masonry anchors is to lock a masonry drill bit into the chuck of a portable electric drill. If you have a drill, or if you can borrow one from a friend, this technique is easier than using a star drill. Before you attach furring to the wall, make sure the wall is dry. If the wall is damp, coat the surface with a quality masonry paint. If the paneling will be applied directly to the masonry with adhesive, the walls must also be dry.

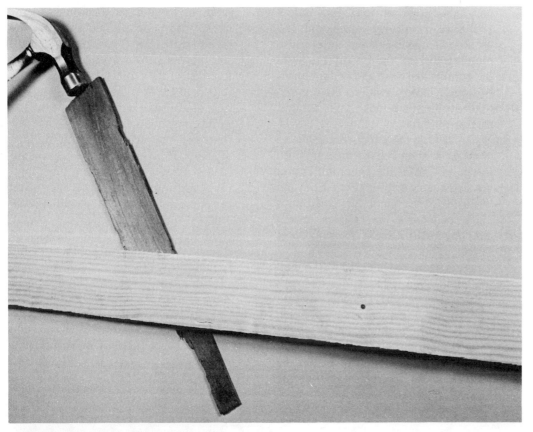

Cedar shingle shims may be used under the furring strips to level the panel-fastening surface. If you still need furring strips for the paneling job even though the wall is fairly straight, you can fasten the strips to the wall with builder's or panel adhesive. When you can, put up the furring strips so that the grain in the wood runs vertically with the panel. You can use 1 by 3 or 1 by 4 boards for furring, or you can cut furring strips out of plywood in this size.

Wall panel application

In this section, we will explain the techniques of applying wall paneling. If the wall surface has been properly prepared, the panels will go up quickly.

If you are going to put panels over furring strips, the following information is important.

1. The panel edges should join over a furring strip or split the width of a stud—¾-inch with an overlap (studs are 1½ inches thick).

2. Use 3d finishing nails to fasten the panels. Space the nails about 6 inches apart along the edges of the panels. Along the furring strips, space the nails 12 inches apart. When you can, nail the paneling in the grooves. You can hide the nailheads by countersinking them slightly and by filling the holes with a special putty stick you can buy for this job. The stick comes in various colors to match the paneling color.

3. Nail the panels at the top and bottom with 6d or 8d (penny) finishing nails. The baseboard and crown molding will hide these nails.

4. To allow for expansion and contraction of the panels, leave $\frac{1}{16}$ inch between each panel. Leave ¼ inch between the bottom of the panel and the flooring. Leave ⅛ inch between the panel and the ceiling. When you use the adhesive method to fasten panels, you should also have the same spacing.

5. If you are nailing the paneling over studs, use 6d nails and space them according to the above schedule. Countersink the nailheads, and fill the nail holes with a putty stick.

6. You can precut the panels to fit for both the nail and the adhesive fastening method. However, we suggest cutting and fitting the panels as you put them up. This technique leaves less margin for error.

7. Wall paneling may be mitered at inside and outside corners; this makes a

very slick-looking job. But unless you have the proper equipment and are knowledgeable about miters, use molding to hide the imperfections at the corners and base and ceiling lines. Mitering, in our opinion, is very difficult to do since most walls are not true or plumb.

8. When sawing the panels for fit, use a crosscut saw and make the cuts with the good side of the panel up. If you are using a power saw, cut from the back side of the panel. Never use a rip blade or coarse saw blades to cut paneling. Also, measure twice; cut once.

9. Depending on the pattern, wall paneling may be installed either horizontally or vertically on the wall surface. The material can also be installed both vertically and horizontally in the same room to produce interesting patterns. But before you do this, make sure that you have worked out the patterns to your satisfaction.

10. Panel only one wall to start; let the job sit overnight. The next day, check the panels before you continue with the rest of the project. The purpose of this is to see how the panels are adapting to the wall surface. Some of the joints may contract. If so, you need to butt the next series of joints tighter. There can be considerable expansion and contraction in wooden paneling.

11. When fitting ⅛-inch thick, V-grooved paneling, handle the small pieces carefully. The thickness between the bottom of the groove and the back of the panel is extremely thin, and the panel may break at the groove. You don't have to be concerned about large pieces, only those 15 inches or less in length. In this section, we have also included information on the adhesive technique of panel installation.

Spread the adhesive all over the wall. But don't overdo it, especially at the panel joints and the floor and ceiling line where the adhesive can ooze from the joints. Spread adhesive on one panel at a time; don't do an entire wall. Set the panel in position at the ceiling line, and press it in place. Then pull the panel away from the wall at the bottom. This helps spread the beads of adhesive on the wall and on the panel back. Next, press the panel into permanent position. Nail the panel along the vertical joints at the top and at the bottom. Then tap the panel surface with a piece of scrap wood covered with a towel for padding. This also helps to spread the adhesive evenly.

Cuts for electrical outlets, registers, and around windows and doors are made after you measure the wall and transfer the measurement to the back of the panel. Although the switch and outlet plate and the flange around the registers will cover slight imperfections, measure as accurately as possible. To make a pocket cut, scribe the outline of the pocket on the panel. Then bore a hole at one corner of the outline, as shown. The bit (or drill) should be within the scribed lines. Double-check your measurements before you bore a hole.

Make the pocket cut in the panel with a keyhole saw or a power saber saw. When you are finished, try to fit the panel over the electrical outlet. If the cut is slightly off, the cover plate may compensate for the error. If you are badly out of alignment, you will probably have to cut another panel; it would be almost impossible to patch the error.

Separated vertical joints in paneling often are caused by contraction of the panels after they are in position on the wall. Most of the problem can be eliminated by letting the panels sit in the room several days before you apply them to the wall. This should allow the paneling to adjust to the humidity. However, moisture is tricky, and the panels may contract. If so, wait until the panels have been in place about a week; then spray the cracks with black flat enamel. This will hide the separated joints.

Immediately wipe off the excess enamel. Start at the bottom of the V-groove and work up. You probably will not be able to wipe off all the enamel with the first swipe. Lightly soak a cloth pad in paint thinner and go over the panel, removing all the excess enamel. You don't have to rub hard. Also, be careful that you don't remove the fresh paint from the V-groove.

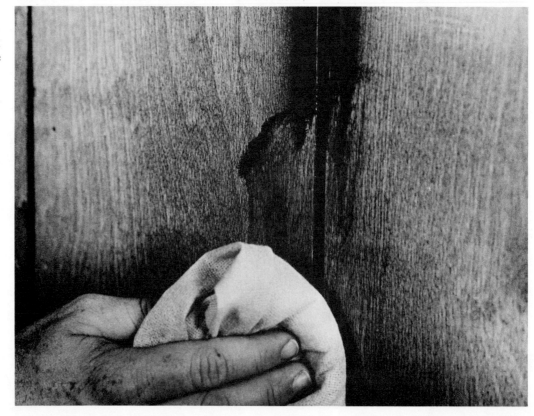

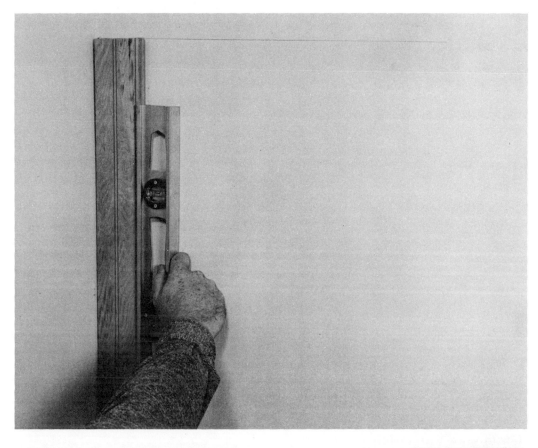

Solid wood paneling comes in various widths and thicknesses. It may be applied to furring strips or directly to the wall, as explained earlier. The trick is to match the various panels for grain variation before you install each panel. All of the same techniques—furring, wall preparation, and adhesive—apply to solid wood paneling as you would apply to plywood and hardboard paneling. Make sure the first piece of paneling you apply is plumb (vertically level). You can use a carpenter's level for this, as shown. As you apply the individual panels, check the plumb about every three to four panels to make sure they are being put on the wall straight and true.

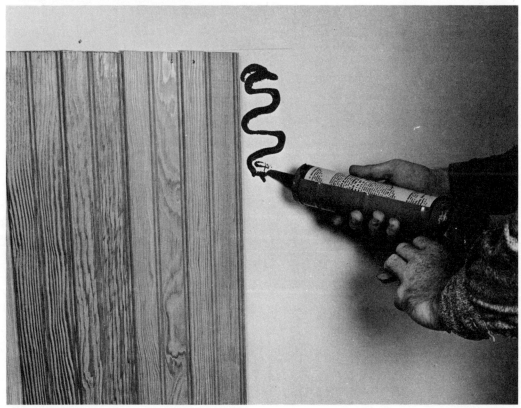

Panel adhesive is applied this way. Use plenty of adhesive, and apply just one panel at a time. After the panel is up, pull it away from the wall and stick the panel down again. This spreads the adhesive. Then nail the panel to the studs in back of the wall or to the furring strips. If the panels have tongue-and-groove joints, you don't have to nail every panel.

Electrical outlets are designed so that you can adjust them to be flush with the wall surface. You will probably have to put two small wooden shims behind the "ears" of the outlet where it screws into the metal junction box. You will have to experiment with this. Put the outlet cover on the switch to make sure the unit is flush with the wall paneling. While you work, turn off the power at the main circuit breaker or fuse box.

How to work with moldings

A miter box and a backsaw are necessary to cut molding and trim properly. A miter box has slots that are used to cut moldings at right and left 45-degree angles, and it has a 90-degree slot for straight cuts. You can buy a miter box with a special saw holder; this will lock the saw so that it can't slip. If you buy the saw holder, cut miters about 1 degree less than the above measurement—44 degrees instead of 45 degrees. This small difference will make the joint tighter when you assemble it.

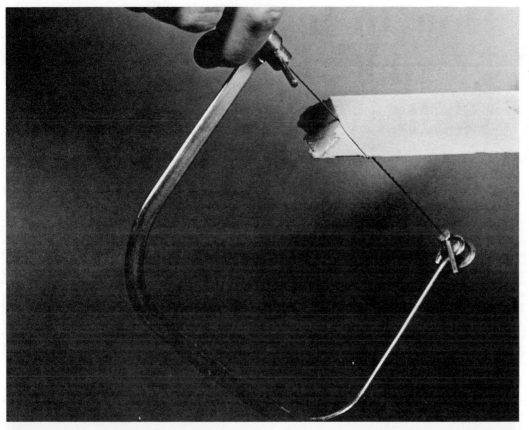

Joints have to be coped (to notch or cut away a part of)—especially base shoe joints—so that the pieces fit together tightly. To do this, turn the 2 metal pins where the blade connects to the saw frame. Then guide the saw blade around the contour of the molding, as shown. When you are finished, the cut should fit the contour of the matching molding perfectly. However, if the molding is slightly off, you can fit it with a razor knife, cutting away any excess wood.

Cut molding to fit by installing one piece of molding; then carefully mark the miter cut on the adjoining piece of molding, as shown. When measuring long lengths of molding, have a helper hold the molding while you mark it. This assures accuracy. We recommend that you finish unfinished molding before you install the material. This is easier than trying to stain the molding after it is fastened to the wall. You may have to touch up saw cuts and nailheads with stain later, but this is still easier than staining the entire job.

How to Install Flexible Wallcoverings

Since wallpaper is not always made of paper now, the word wallcovering is used; it applies to a variety of materials. We've added the word flexible to wallcoverings to differentiate from wall paneling, ceramic tile, simulated brick and stone, and all the other rigid materials on the market.

In our opinion, flexible wallcoverings are not as easy to apply as wall paneling, but they are certainly within your skills.

Types of wallcoverings include vinyl, foil, flocked foil, burlap, fabric, and strawgrass. You may buy wallcoverings that are trimmed, untrimmed, prepasted, and ready-to-paste. The wallcoverings may also have a paper or a cloth backing.

Most flexible wallcoverings are manufactured in rolls that are 27 inches wide. You can buy some wallcoverings in rolls that are 54 inches wide. The wider products are most difficult to hang because of the width.

The most popular do-it-yourself wallcoverings today probably are the so-called, vinyl-faced products. The surface of the paper is washable. Also, the vinyls are resistant to fading and to household stains.

Some wallcoverings—burlap, hand-painted murals, foils, and hand prints—require a lining paper for the best results. The lining will add to the cost, but this material provides a cushion for the wallcovering, and you get a smoother job.

You can buy flexible wallcoverings trimmed or untrimmed. If this is your first wallcovering project, we suggest that you buy trimmed paper. It's easier to hang. We also suggest that you use a simple pattern that is easily matched for your first project.

You can change the look of a room with flexible wallcoverings. If you use a wallcovering with a horizontal pattern, a narrow room will look wider. If you want a low ceiling to look higher, buy a wallcovering that has a vertical pattern. If you want the room to look larger, buy a light-colored wallcovering. If you want the room to look smaller, buy a dark-colored wallcovering.

Wallcovering types and hanging tips

In this chapter you will find specific instructions on hanging the modern wallcoverings. Basically, all wallcoverings are installed the same way with a few variations. Here is a list of specific wallcoverings and tips on hanging them.

Lining paper

Use lining paper for foils, hand prints, burlaps, and murals. If you can afford it, use lining paper for all wallcoverings. (See the illustrations in this chapter.)

Lining paper is installed with presized wheat paste. If you are applying the liner to a wall that has been painted with a semigloss paint, mix a combination of one part vinyl adhesive to three parts wheat paste.

Never overlap lining paper. Although you should try to butt the joints tightly, you can leave gaps at the seams of the paper. Lining paper should be installed over walls that have been prepared properly.

Prepasted wallcoverings

You do not have to add paste to prepasted wallcoverings. This material hangs best on walls that are porous or semiporous. If your old wallpaper is in good condition, you can apply new paper over it.

Make sure the prepasted rolls soak in water for a fairly long time or according to the manufacturer's recommendations. When you hang the paper, be careful that you do not stretch it on the wall. The paper tends to shrink slightly when it dries.

Machine printed wallcoverings

If the paper is printed on a strippable backing, the joints may be difficult to fit together since the paper is heavy and doesn't absorb much moisture. You can't push and shape the paper on the wall easily.

As a rule, you should paste only one length of this paper at a time; then immediately hang it on the wall. Use wheat paste and thoroughly cover the backing. After you hang a strip, sponge down the joint or seam with water. This will remove any dried paste.

If the wallcovering has a metallic dye in it, the paste can cause discoloring of the surface. To prevent this, stir two tablespoons of borax into each batch of paste and two tablespoons of borax into the clear rinsing water.

Use a seam roller to firmly press the seams of the wallcovering against the wall. Run the roller back a little way from the seam. If you roll just the seam, the paper may stretch here; then it may shrink back when the paste dries.

Vinyl wallcovering with a paper backing

We recommend this wallcovering because it is pretrimmed with a machine-printed face. The paper is fairly easy to hang; you can also remove the covering easily when you want to redecorate the room.

If you buy a paper-backed, hand-printed vinyl wallcovering, you will have to trim the paper at the selvages.

To hang the paper-backed vinyl papers, use plenty of adhesive; make sure you cover the backing smoothly and evenly. Too little adhesive makes the paper difficult to hang. If there is not enough adhesive on the surface, the paper may curl at the seams and at the ceiling and floor line. Without the proper adhesive, the paper won't slip, and it will be hard to work out the air bubbles under the paper.

Be careful not to stretch vinyl paper as you hang it. If the seams curl after the paper has been hung, try sticking the seams down with vinyl-to-vinyl adhesive.

Vinyl wallcovering with a cloth backing

This material can be stiff; a big advantage is that the covering is strippable. You may easily take the paper off whenever you want to redecorate.

We recommend that you use a wheat paste for adhesive; paste several strips at a time.

If you hang a heavyweight vinyl wallcovering in a 45- to 57-inch width, use a premixed vinyl adhesive. When you store this wallcovering, do not stand the rolls on end; you may damage the seams.

When you go around a corner with the heavyweight material, lap it about 6 to 8 inches around the corner. This will help prevent the seam from opening when the adhesive dries.

Flocked vinyl wallcoverings

When hanging this material, keep the paste off the flocked surface. If paste does get on the surface, gently wash it off with clear water. Dry the surface by blotting it with a clean cloth. If the flock is matted, you can reactivate it by brushing the flock with a suede shoe brush.

Vinyl wallcoverings with a wet look

These papers are fairly easy to hang. However, you must prepare the wall surface properly. If there are any ridges, drips, or lumps on the wall surface, the imperfections will show through the paper.

Metal foil wallcoverings

We recommend a lining paper for metal foil wallcoverings. If the foil has a cloth backing, you do not have to line the walls.

When you hang foil papers, be careful around electrical outlets. The foil is a conductor of electricity, and you could get a shock. Turn off the electricity at the main circuit breaker or fuse box when you cut and trim foil around electrical switches and outlets.

Burlap

Paper-backed burlap probably is the most popular wallcovering today; it is easy to use since you can butt the seams. Also, it is fairly easy to paste and to trim.

Be careful not to set the rolls on edge when you store them; the weight of the roll can damage the edges. We recommend that you use a liner with burlap. Use powdered vinyl adhesive to hang the material, but do not use too much water to mix it. Most authorities agree that you should mix the adhesive with about ½ pint less water than the instructions on the package recommend. Also, it is recommended that you apply the adhesive with a mohair roller instead of a brush. Give the surface two coats of adhesive. You will notice that the first coat will seem to absorb into the backing. The second coat will give you plenty of adhesive to hang the paper.

The texture of simulated or printed burlap is not as sharp as that of regular burlap; printed burlap is usually paper backed.

Cloth

You can hang regular fabrics—even sheet material. The key is to apply vinyl adhesive directly to the wall and not to the material. The material tends to stretch when it becomes moist from the adhesive. Therefore, you have to be careful not to stretch it, or the seams will pull apart when the adhesive dries.

The adhesive has to be applied smoothly. Use plenty of it on the wall surface—over a lining if your budget permits—and brush out all of the air bubbles with a wall brush.

Grass cloth

You'll probably buy the cellulose type rather than the natural grass cloth. The cellulose type comes in rolls 36 inches wide by 24 feet long (double roll); from each double roll, you will get three 8-foot strips.

Cellulose grass cloth tends to stretch, so you should measure from the floor to the ceiling and cut the piece this size.

Use wheat paste, and try not to get adhesive on the face of the paper. You may smear some adhesive on it; remove this adhesive immediately with a dry, soft cloth or a towel.

When you apply the strips, use a seam roller and softly press the seams to the wall. Otherwise, you will press the fibers into the wall, and the seams will show.

The seams may lose their vertical plumb when you hang the pieces. If so, try pulling the paper on the outside edge and stretching this edge down the wall. If the strip tends to

overlap, pull the paper downward on the butt edge side. It will align properly.

Cork-faced paper

This wallcovering tends to curl when you hang it on the wall. It is best to use a liner.

Mix wheat paste with one part vinyl adhesive to four parts of wheat adhesive. Cover the entire backing with adhesive.

Cork papers are randomly matched. You can't repeat the pattern. Therefore, check the match before the strips are pasted down on the wall. Immediately after the strips are hung, you should roll the seams lightly. The paper tends to stretch. If you damage a section of the paper, wait until it dries. Then go back, cut a patch, and paste the patch over the damaged area. Roll the seams. The patch won't show if you match the pattern.

Adhesives

When you buy a specific wallcovering—vinyl, foil, or burlap—the sales person often will recommend the right kind of adhesive for it. Below is a list of adhesives, and it includes the type of wallcovering that may be used with each adhesive.

Wheat paste vinyl adhesive

Use this adhesive for lightweight vinyls. The adhesive has a slow drying time under heavy vinyl wallcoverings; this could cause mildew.

Vinyl-to-vinyl adhesive

This paste usually won't adhere to itself. Use it at the seams or joints of vinyl wallcovering.

Wheat paste

Buy the self-sizing type for a good bond. Sizing is a material used to seal the wall surface. Many adhesives include sizing. Wheat paste works best on uncoated wallcoverings.

Powder vinyl adhesive

Use this adhesive for hanging paper-backed vinyl and the heavy wallcoverings. It is tacky and will not mold. We recommend that you use a medium-napped paint roller to apply the adhesive. Also, you should size (seal) a porous wall with four parts water to one part paste. Do not use a powder vinyl adhesive over a highly sealed surface. And, if the room is subject to high humidity, do not use this adhesive.

Cellulose adhesive

This adhesive is ideal to use with a shikii silk wallcovering over a lining paper. Mix the adhesive in a plastic pail because it will corrode galvanized steel buckets.

Do not intermix adhesives without testing them first. You can do this by attaching a small piece of wallcovering with the adhesive mixture onto the wall you want to cover. Let the mixture dry at least overnight before you make a decision.

Wall Preparation

Before hanging almost any wallcovering, you must prepare a wall surface properly. If there are nicks, cracks, and holes in the wall surface, these imperfections will show through the wallcovering.

Preparing walls for wallcoverings is a time-consuming job; it takes patience. But the result will be a smooth wallcovering surface, and this is important.

Preparing walls for wallcoverings is not a difficult job technically. You will need a wide wall scraper and/or a putty knife, spackling compound, a bucket, medium-grit sandpaper, and a wooden sanding block (can be formed from a piece of scrap wood).

Gypsum wallboard and lath-and-plaster walls are repaired almost the same way; there are no special techniques involved.

If the wall you will cover is painted, make sure the wall is free of grease. Trisodium phosphate dissolved in water is a compound that may be used to remove grease.

If the paint on the wall is peeling, you should remove it. If the problem is severe, scratch off the paint with a scraper and cover the walls with lining paper.

If the wall is painted with a glossy paint, go over the surface with steel wool to dull the gloss. Paper sticks better to a dull surface.

If the wall has a sand finish, go over the surface with a wide scraper. Then lightly sand the wall and cover it with a lining paper.

Wallpapered walls

You may put new wallpaper over old wallpaper if the old paper is well bonded to the wall. If not, we recommend that you remove the paper. A wallpaper steamer is the best method; a chemical remover is the second best method—in our opinion.

New plaster/gypsum wallboard walls

Give these surfaces a coat of sealer. For plaster walls, brush on a coat of this solution: one pound of zinc sulphate in one gallon of water. When the solution dries, rinse the walls with clear water, and wait 10 days before you apply wallcovering.

Wallcoverings over plywood

If the plywood has random grooves, you should cover them with a fiber glass tape. All of the nicks and nailheads should be filled with spackling compound, and the spackling should be sanded smooth with a medium-grit abrasive. Then, give the wall a coat of penetrating sealer.

Glue sizing

You usually do not have to size walls, because the manufacturers of wallcovering adhesive have put the sizing in the adhesive.

You may have to use a glue size with wallcoverings that require paste as an adhesive. However, this should be discussed with your wallcovering dealer. It depends on the wall, the adhesive, and the wallcovering.

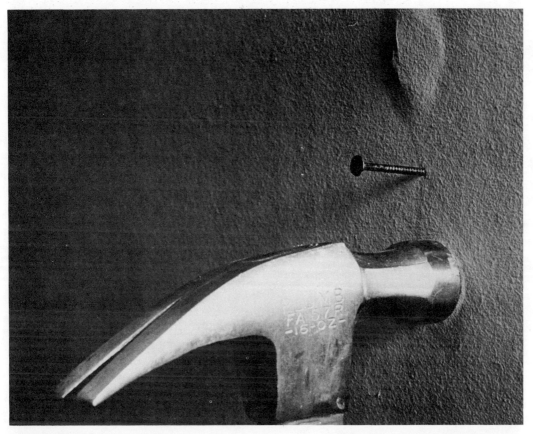

Nail pops in gypsum wallboard are common. They are caused by your home's settling on its foundation, and moisture. The pops have to be eliminated because they will show through most flexible wallcoverings. Hit the pop with a hammer, slightly denting the gypsum wallboard. Then, right above or below the pop, drive a threaded gypsum board nail into the framing member. This usually prevents the nails from popping again. Fill the indentations left by the hammerhead with spackling compound. Let the spackling dry, and then sand the wall surface smooth.

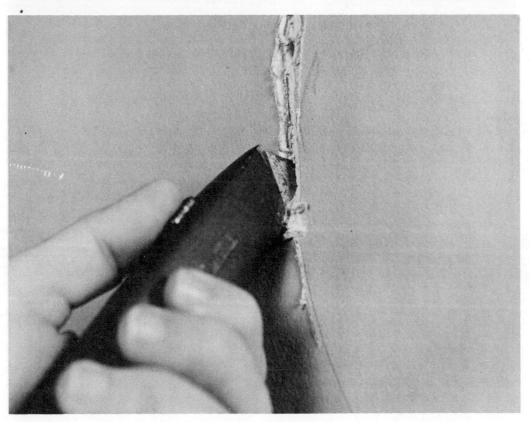

Hairline cracks around doors and windows, and sometimes on large wall surfaces, are caused by the house's settling on its foundation. This is normal, unless the cracks are especially large. If the cracks are especially large, consult a builder. There may be structural damage to your home. Otherwise, fill the hairline cracks by cleaning them out, as shown, with a razor knife. If the wall is made of gypsum wallboard, sand the surface lightly with a medium-grit abrasive over a sanding block. This will remove the excess paper covering over the gypsum wallboard core. You want a smooth surface.

Fill the crack with spackling compound. The spackling, mixed with water, should be the consistency of stiff whipped cream. Force the spackling into the crack with a stiff-bladed putty knife or a wall scraper. Leave the spackling slightly high in the crack; the spackling will shrink slightly when it dries. Try to remove all excess spackling around the crack with the tip of the putty knife or scraper. This will make it easier to sand the spackling when it dries.

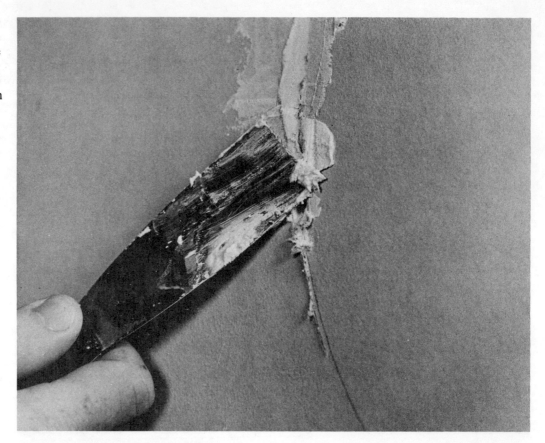

Sand the hairline crack after the spackling dries; let it dry about 3 hours. However, if you can, let the spackling compound dry overnight before sanding. Use a sanding block. The block is flat so that you don't dig the abrasive into the wall as you sand. Use a medium-grit abrasive—open coat. Go easy; spackling is soft.

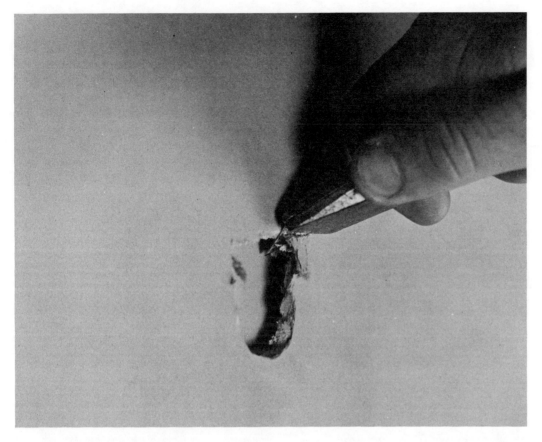

Small holes in gypsum wallboard (and lath and plaster) can be repaired with steel wool and spackling compound. First, trim away the broken plaster or gypsum wallboard, as shown. Use a razor knife, and remove all of the loose material. The edges of the break have to be solid.

Stuff the hole with fairly coarse steel wool. The steel wool will cling to the edges of the hole without support. Then tack (or hold) the steel wool in position with spackling compound. The compound should be fairly stiff; don't use too much water when you mix it. Wipe compound around the edges with a putty knife, and let this dry overnight. Then fill in the patch with spackling compound. Fill the patch overly full, since the spackling shrinks when it dries. When the patch is dry, lightly sand it with a medium-grit abrasive over a sanding block.

If you have a large hole in gypsum wallboard—3 inches square or more—you can buy a special kit to cover the hole. The kit consists of a piece of gypsum wallboard material, special clips, a little saw, and spackling compound. You put the patch over the hole, as shown, and pencil the outline of the patch on the wall. This provides you with a cutting guideline.

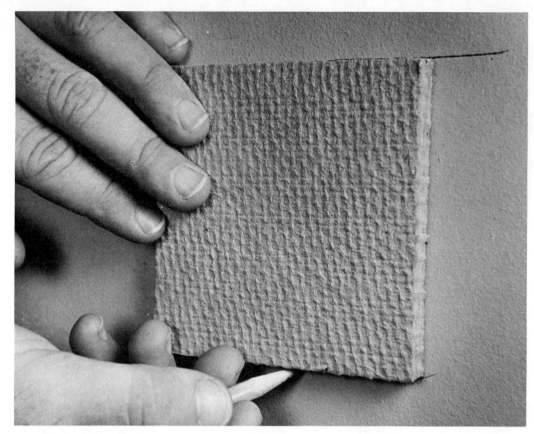

Saw out the damaged area using the patch guidelines. Make the cut as smooth and square as you can, since the patch has to fit into this area. If you have a scrap piece of gypsum wallboard around the house, you can make a homemade patch.

Special clips made of plastic are inserted at the 4 edges of the gypsum wallboard. The clips are designed to fit various thicknesses of gypsum board; you break off tiny plastic tabs to the correct thickness of the wallboard material. Make sure the clips are firmly in place.

Snap the patch into position. The special plastic clips will hold the patch firmly. If the hole hasn't been cut properly, you can use a rasp or coarse file to trim away the excess gypsum wallboard. Or, you can trim the patch to fit. However, we recommend that you trim the wallboard. It is easier.

Cover the patch with spackling compound. The patch will be somewhat recessed in the wall. Mix the spackling compound slightly stiff; overfill the patch slightly, since the spackling will shrink when it dries. Let the patch dry for at least 1 day. Then sand the patch smooth with a medium-grit abrasive on a sanding block. For larger holes, we suggest that you remove the entire sheet of gypsum wallboard and replace it. The board is fastened to the studs with nails. You will have to cut the taped joints, remove the nails and the board, and apply the new board. Then retape the joints.

If the walls are already covered with wallcovering, you can apply new wallcovering over the old. However, the old wallcovering must be tight on the wall. The old wallcovering may have tiny imperfections. If so, remove the excess paper; then sand or feather the edges smooth. Use a fine-grit abrasive for this, and be careful not to dig into the wall. You want a smooth area over which to put the new wallcovering.

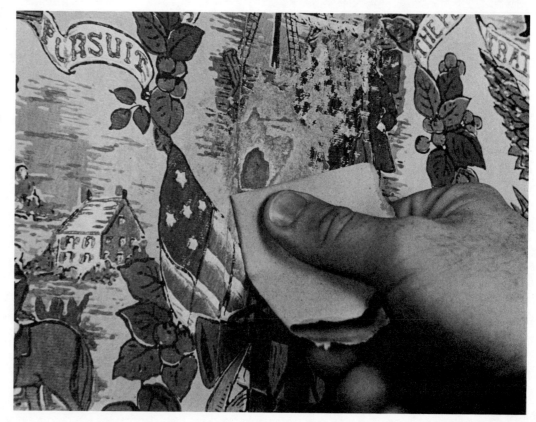

If the wallcovering is loose on the wall, you should remove it. This is a job. In our opinion, the best way to remove the paper is with a wallpaper steamer. You can rent this equipment (usually about $15 per day) at rental outlets and at some wallcovering outlets. The equipment consists of a steam-generating boiler (which usually operates on electricity), a hose, and a wall plate through which the steam flows. The steam loosens the wallcovering so that you can remove it. If the existing wallcovering is strippable, you can simply pull it off the wall. Before you rent a steamer, find out what type of wallcovering you have.

A chemical wallpaper remover is mixed with water and sponged over the wallcovering. It is important that the chemical has enough time to soak through the surface into the adhesive. Do not be in a rush to remove the paper with a wall scraper. You may also use a chemical remover in a garden sprayer. Spray the wall several times, let the chemical work, and remove the paper with a scraper. The big drawback with a chemical remover is the water that ends up on the floor. Also, a chemical remover takes longer to work than a wallpaper steamer does. However, using the chemical remover is less expensive than using the steamer. If you use the chemical method, be sure to clean up the water as you work to avoid damage to the floor.

The Basics of Hanging Wallcoverings

When you hang wallcoverings, be systematic. Do first things first, and pay attention to detail. If you do this, the project will be successful, and you will be happy with the job. There are no shortcuts, but there are little tips that will make the job go smoother.

The illustrations show most of these tips. However, we want to explain several of them, even if we are redundant.

- Hang the first strip of wallpaper next to a door, window, or at the end of a wall. Always work toward the longest wall in the room that does not have a doorway or a window in it.
- If you are hanging a wallcovering with a large pattern, paste on the first strips at a point of interest in the room—such as a fireplace wall. This should be your starting point for the rest of the room.
- There are two methods that may be used to join the seams or joints of wallcovering: butt or lap. It is easier to butt the seams than to lap them. Also, if the wallcovering is pretrimmed, a butt seam is the best to use.
- To make the job easier:
  1. Remove the furnishings or put them in the center of the room.
  2. Properly prepare the wall surface.
  3. Organize your tools and materials so that they are handy.
  4. Work slowly.
  5. Keep things clean as you work. If you spill paste on the floor, wipe it up immediately. This also applies to wall preparation. Sweep up chunks of gypsum wallboard, sawdust, and other debris.

The illustrations and text in this chapter apply to almost all wallcoverings and to special wallcoverings such as foil and burlap. It is important that you use your common sense when you hang wallcoverings.

Adhesive or paste should be mixed according to the manufacturer's recommendations on the package. The type of paste you will use depends on the wallcovering; this has been explained in the section on adhesives. As a general rule, we recommend that you add the paste to the water in a bucket—not the water to the paste. Use a putty knife, as shown, for mixing the adhesive, or a wooden paddle. Press the lumps of adhesive against the sides of the bucket and stir the mixture until it is perfectly smooth—like whipped cream.

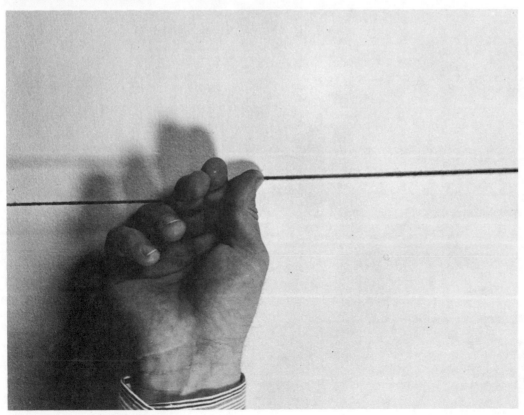

With a plumb bob and a chalk line, snap a vertical line next to a door, window, or at the end of a predominant wall. Hang the plumb bob and the chalk line on a nail. Let the line become motionless. Then, hold the chalk line taut at the bottom, and snap it with your fingers. This will leave a line on the wall that establishes the plumb, or true vertical. *You must use this technique before you apply any flexible wallcovering to the wall.*

Measure and cut about 3 to 6 lengths of wallcovering, unless you are using a special wallcovering (which is explained in this chapter). The strips should be about 2 inches longer than the measurement from the floor to the ceiling. This gives you extra material for matching and trimming. Apply plenty of adhesive to the backing—especially along the edges. Look at the strips in the light to make sure you don't have any dry spots on the backing. Adhesive must cover the entire backing.

Put paste on half the length of the strip. Then fold this half over, as shown. Now paste the other half (not in photograph) the same way and fold it over. Do not crease the paper at the fold line. Have plenty of fold. If you crease the paper, it will show, when you put the paper on the wall.

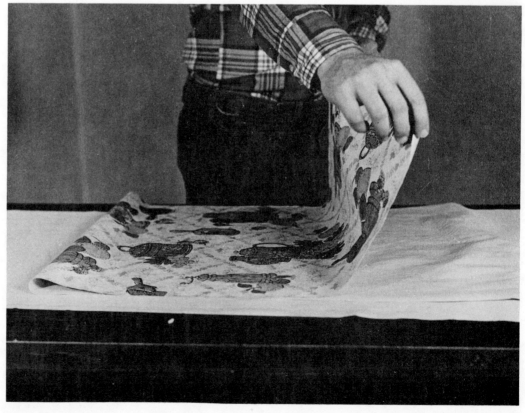

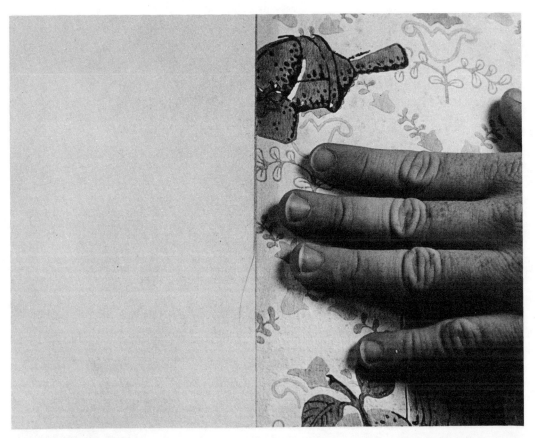

Apply the top half of the first strip to the wall, butting the seam or joint against the true vertical or plumb line. The adhesive will make the paper slick so that you can slide it on the wall. *This first strip must be true vertical.* If the strip is not vertical, the error will be compounded in the rest of the strips that you hang. You will have an excess of paper at the ceiling and at the floor line; this paper will be trimmed later. Immediately use the smoothing brush to brush the paper so that it fits tightly to the wall. Now, unfold the bottom half of the strip, and brush it tightly against the wall.

Hit the brush hard against the wallcovering. The pressure or pounding works out the wrinkles and the air bubbles in the paper. First stroke the brush down the center of the strip. Then move the brush out toward the seams. This will help remove the air bubbles and the wrinkles. If you can't remove a wrinkle or an air bubble, lift the paper from the bottom and smooth it down again with the smoothing brush. Do not be reluctant to do this; the adhesive does not dry immediately.

Lap the corner seam about 2 inches past the corner. Tap the paper into the corner with the smoothing brush. Tap hard so that the paper fits snugly into the corner. The seam that laps around the corner will probably not be plumb or vertically level. Don't worry. You can usually lap—not butt—the next strip of paper, and the seam will not show. Also, you can double cut the seam; we show how to do this later.

Use the seam roller to press down the seams, after you have applied three strips of wallcovering. If the seams are curling, you have not put enough adhesive on the backing. You can add more adhesive with a small paintbrush. Use enough paste at the outset, and be sure to cover the edges of the strips adequately. At this point, you should also trim off the excess paper at the ceiling line and at the floor; use a razor knife. Work from the center of the strip out to the edges. If you tear the paper, it can easily be patched by slipping the ragged edges into place or by cutting a small patch out of scrap.

Clean off the adhesive from the face of the wall-covering as you hang each strip. Use clear water and a sponge for this, and change the water frequently. Do not be afraid to apply plenty of clear water to the paper's surface. The water will not harm the paper. Move the sponge over the paper easily; don't rub hard.

You may have to slit the wallcovering in the corners because they may not be plumb. Do this whenever the paper does not adhere firmly to the surface. Then use the smoothing brush to push down paper. You will have to do this with thick wallcoverings. When you are hanging vinyl papers, adjust the strip to the vertical plumb line. You should apply just enough pressure to stick the strip to the wall. The seam should be butted from the ceiling to the floor. Use the seam roller on the seam, as suggested above, after you have applied three strips of wallcovering.

This technique is called double cutting. Place one piece of wallcovering over another piece of wallcovering. This produces a lapped joint. Then put a straightedge over both pieces, and plumb the overlapped strip. Cut the strip with a razor knife. Then peel off the strip on top that you have cut; lift the lapped edge and peel off the strip that is left underneath. The strips that are left should form a butt seam. The razor knife must be extremely sharp, and you must move quickly. Determine the vertical level with the straightedge, and quickly pull the knife down the edge.

Snap a chalk line to make the lining paper plumb. The seams or joints of the paper should not be overlapped. In fact, you don't even have to butt them together tightly. When you hang this material, trim ⅛ inch below the ceiling line, baseboards, and door and window casings. Make sure that the lining does not have air bubbles in the corners. Do this by cutting the liner with a razor knife.

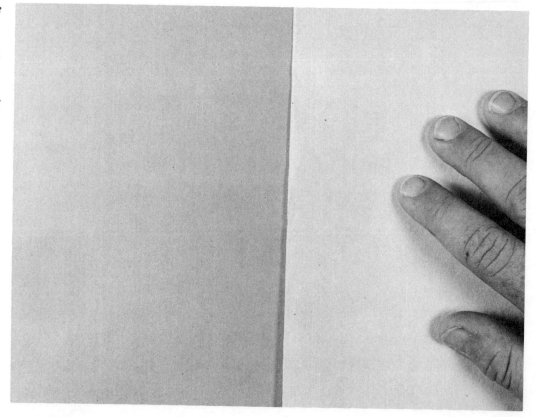

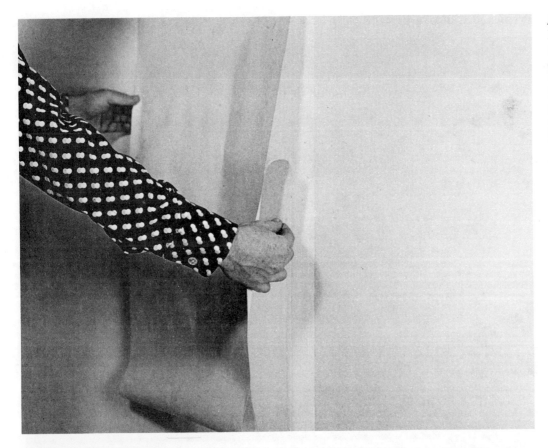

Put paste on the lining paper. Fold the paper twice, apply it to the wall at the ceiling, and drop it down the wall as shown. You can fill in any gaps—over doors and windows—after you have the basic strips in position.

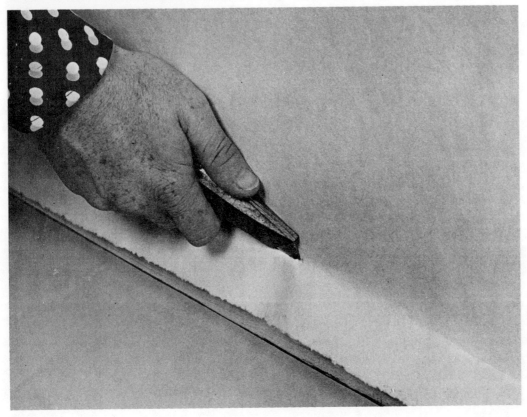

Trim the lining paper from the middle to the outer edges at the baseboard and ceiling. You have to be fast with the razor knife so that you do not tear the paper. You can also cut the paper with scissors. If you use scissors, start at one edge and cut to the other edge of the paper. When the blades of the scissors become encrusted with adhesive, wash them off with water and a sponge.

Prepasted wallcoverings

Prepasted wallcoverings often are rolled with the pattern on the outside of the roll. If you buy paper this way, reroll it so that the face of the paper is on the inside of the roll. This is not absolutely necessary; however, you should reroll the paper so that it is loose in the roll, as shown. This permits the water in the water tray to activate the adhesive on the back of the strips.

To hang prepasted paper, pull the sheet up from the water tray to the ceiling. Take a smoothing brush and press the sheet against the wall in the center of the sheet. Move all the way down the strip, and work the brush from the center of the strip toward the sides, removing any air bubbles and wrinkles. If there are any wrinkles or air bubbles, lift the strip from the bottom and rework it on the wall with the smoothing brush.

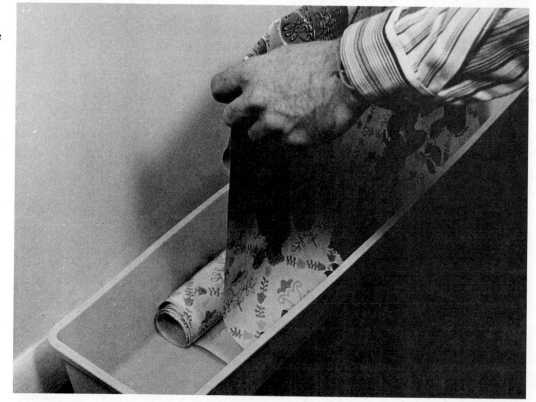

Foils and metallic papers

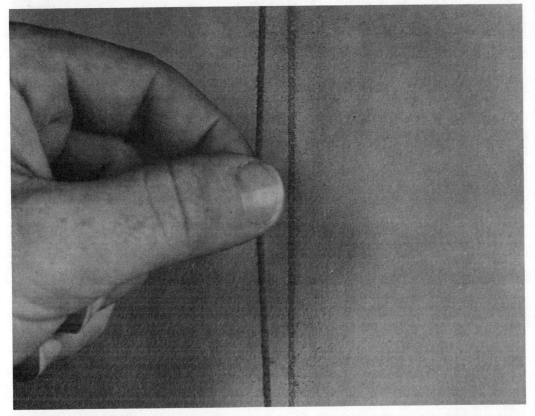

Snap a chalk line on the wall to establish the true vertical plumb. We are reemphasizing this point, because it is important for a professional-looking job. When hanging foil papers, we recommend that you use a liner. The lining paper will make the foil paper fit smoothly; it will also make the foil easier to hang.

Foils may be pretrimmed or untrimmed, as shown. If the rolls are untrimmed, you will have to trim them. The trim points are marked on the rolls, as shown. Some foils have a cloth backing, and these papers do not have to be trimmed. If you buy a foil pattern with a large design, every other strip of paper should usually be reversed so that the pattern will match.

For trimming any paper, you will need a straightedge. They are expensive. We suggest that you buy a length (10 feet) of aluminum angle for a straightedge, as shown. The aluminum is inexpensive (about $6 to $8 for a 10-foot length with a ¾-inch width), and it is rugged. You don't need to worry about bending it out of shape. Aluminum angle can be purchased at most home center stores, hardware outlets, and at general catalog stores.

Use a razor knife to trim papers. You can also use a trimming wheel, but it may be difficult to find at a store. Use a new razor blade in the knife about every 4 rolls of wallcovering. The fabric or foil dulls the razor blade quickly.

Foils have a tendency to curl. To straighten the paper, lay a piece of board over the strip as you trim it. Allow ⅛ inch for the trim. The middle of the strip will be slightly out of alignment on the straight-edge. Put the board on the opposite side of the strip. This should align the trimming points—top, middle, and end. If the strip of foil is longer than 6 feet, trim 3 feet off the edge at a time. This will keep the edge true.

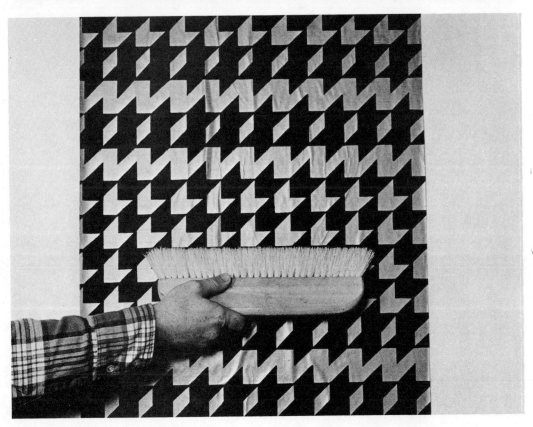

Apply adhesive evenly to the wall with a mohair roller. Use enough paste on the wall to overlap the width of the strip by 3 inches. Apply the paste with a paintbrush at the ceiling and floor lines. Butt the edge of the first strip of foil against the plumb line. Run the smoothing brush down the middle of the strip—from top to bottom—as shown. Use pressure on the brush; you want to push the foil firmly against the wall surface.

Brush from the center to the sides of the strip. This will work out air bubbles and wrinkles. Foil is hard to stick down; you have to press heavily on the smoothing brush. If there are too many air bubbles and wrinkles, pick up the strip from the bottom and reset it. Move the smoothing brush from the center of the strip to the outside edges. After two strips are in place, use the seam roller to roll the seams lightly so that the foil is anchored in position. *Do not press hard on the roller*. Trim the paper at the ceiling line and the base.

The edges of the foil may curl. You may not have used enough adhesive; be sure to use plenty of paste before you start. Even with enough paste, the edges still may curl. If so, hold the edges in place with pins, as shown. The pins should be removed after the adhesive bonds. Burlap and heavy papers also curl. Use the pin technique.

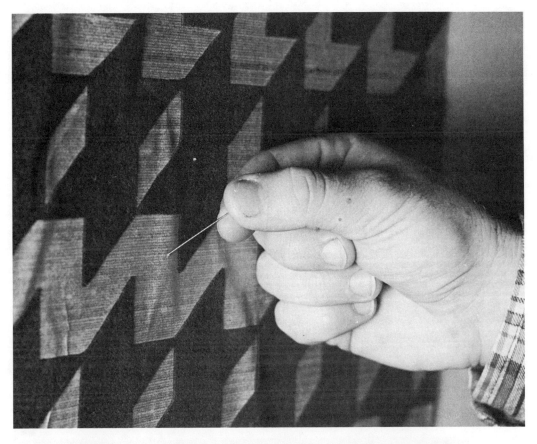

Air bubbles under foil—or under any wallcovering—can be punctured with a pin or a needle. You should try to work these pockets out with the smoothing brush. If you can't, the pin trick works; but be sure to tap the paper down with the smoothing brush after you stick the bubble with the pin.

Bubbles under wallcovering can also be punctured with a razor cut. Make the slit quickly so that you don't tear the paper. This technique can also be used on burlap wallcoverings, but you have to be careful to make the cut between the woven fibers so that the cut doesn't show.

Trimming around electrical outlets, doors, and windows, is no problem. The paper may be mismatched in places; this is common, especially around windows, doors, and fireplaces. Try to keep the pattern of the paper as continuous as you can. However, the last strip you hang may be either several inches short or a full strip wide. You will have to use a full strip here. Cut the strip so that it will extend 1 inch beyond the frame of the door or window. Trim this piece at the casing so that the paper will lay flat on the wall. You now have to cut away—carefully— the excess paper.

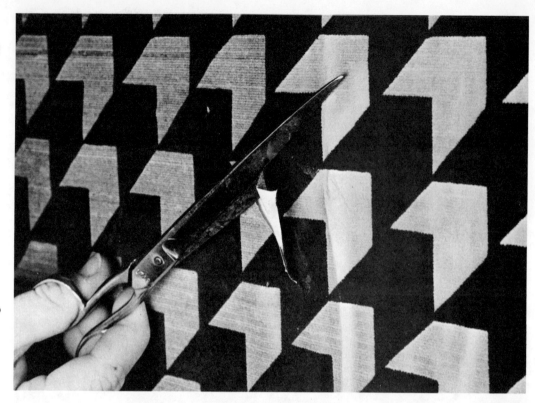

To hang wallpaper on ceilings, you have to have a straight line or a plumb line. You can support the line with thumbtacks, as the drawing shows. Paper the ceiling before you start on the walls. Measure the width of the ceiling paper. Then subtract 1 inch. Put the plumb line 1 inch from the wall at one end of the ceiling. Measure the same width at the other end of the ceiling and place a tack here. The plumb line is snapped at this point. You have to measure the shortest length of the ceiling for the first strip of wallcovering. Add 6 inches to this length and cut all strips to this measurement. The rest of the project is routine—just like covering walls. When you get to the final strip, measure the distance to the wall from the last ceiling strip that you pasted down. Add 1 inch to this. Cut the final strip to this length. After you are finished, trim away the excess paper.

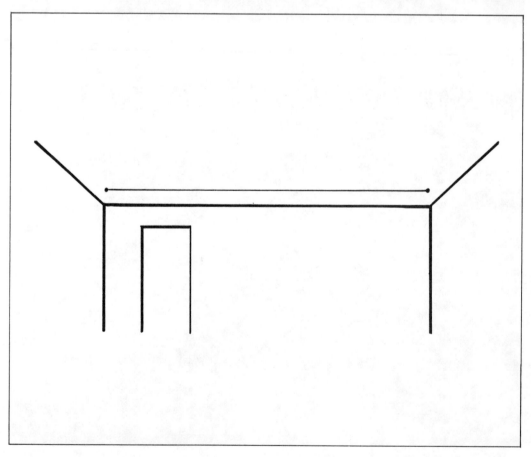

Wallcovering is very heavy to hang on the ceiling. Therefore, you should hang the strips across the ceiling rather than lengthwise. Fold the paper over after you paste it. Then apply the paper to the ceiling, supporting the surplus with a roll of wallcovering, as shown in the drawing. You will have to put the wallcovering on the ceiling and on the walls separately so that the pattern will match properly.

When working with burlap— and other papers with a dropped or matched pattern—number the strips, as shown. The strips must be reversed so that you can match the pattern. Put the numbers at the *top* of the strips—1, 2, 3, 4, 5. Then reverse all even numbers—or odd numbers. You must be careful with burlap wallcoverings. You can snag one of the edges, dislodging a strand of the material. It is very difficult to match the fine hairs of the burlap at the seams or joints.

Spread paste on the wall or on the backing of the burlap. We prefer applying the adhesive to the wall. Use a powdered vinyl paste mixed with water. However, use ½ pint less water than recommended per six-ounce package. This will make the adhesive thicker. With burlap—or any other uncoated wallcovering—you must not use too much water in the adhesive mixture. The water will soak through the burlap and show on the surface. Also, keep the paste off the face of the paper.

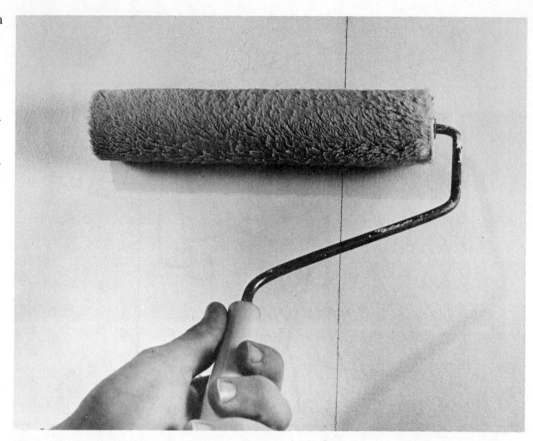

Use a short-napped mohair roller to apply the paste to burlap—either on the wall or on the back of the paper. Make sure you use plenty of adhesive at the edges of the paper. When working with burlap, unroll the material and check it for flaws. If you find a flaw in a roll, you may be able to cut it out of the material. Then, if necessary, you can use the short pieces for patches over doors and windows.

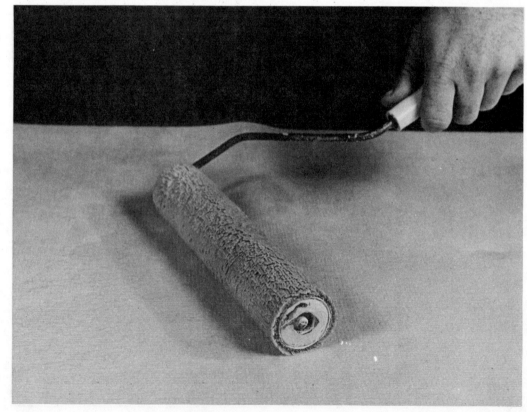

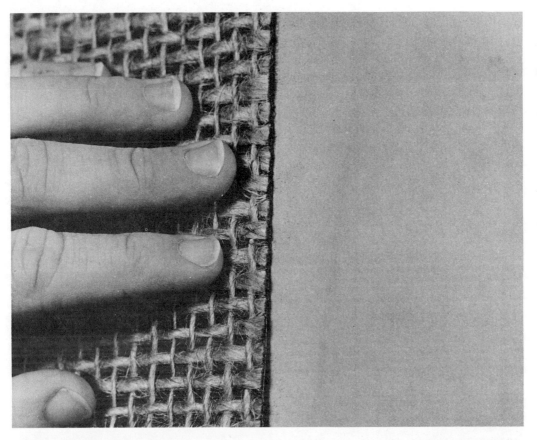

Put the vertical edge of the burlap on the plumb line. Then pull the strip back ⅛ inch, or snap the plumb line ⅛ inch less than the width of the strip. This measurement will help you go around a corner easier when you hang the next strips. Be sure that the room is laid out properly to take advantage of this measurement. With a tape measure, mark the width of the wallcovering around the room from the plumb line. You will be able to determine how the strips will fit in the room.

Match burlap closely. You must also match other wallcoverings, but you usually don't have to be as precise. Put the burlap up against the strip you have just applied to the wall. Check to make sure the threads match. If they don't, you can slide the strip up or down to match. Also, look for snags in this material. If a strand is not aligned properly, the seam will not be matched.

Align the strands of burlap from one sheet to another. You will have to pinch and pull to do this. Press and slip the strips very gently so that the strands align. If the seam is butted too tightly, the little fibers may overlap and lift off the wall. If the seam is not butted closely enough, the wall beneath will show. You must achieve a delicate balance that we can't show you. You will simply have to work with the material until the seams are right.

Lightly roll the seams. Too much pressure will crush the burlap fibers, and the seams will show. The strips should be smoothed both vertically and horizontally, but you should be careful that the smoothing brush does not hit the seam edges. Try to work the smoothing brush within a 3-foot area.

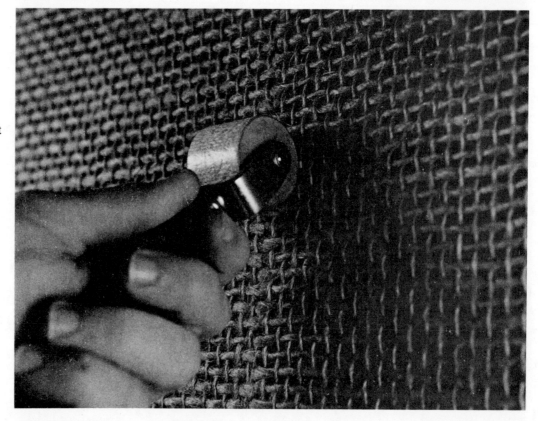

Strands of burlap will work up at the seams. This will call attention to the seams. The strands can be flattened by applying vinyl-to-vinyl adhesive to them with a small artist's brush.
You will have to work carefully to get the fibers in the proper position. After you apply the adhesive, press the fibers down with your fingers. Do not use a roller. The roller can pick up the fibers again, since it holds excess adhesive.

If the edges of the seam tend to curl, you can hold them down with pins as shown. Make sure there is enough adhesive on the paper so that it will stick to the wall. You may have to add adhesive to the backing with a small artist's brush after the covering is on the wall. If so, be careful with the adhesive; you do not want to smear it on the face of the burlap.

When you trim burlap, try to cut the material between the strands. This will prevent the material from unraveling. You should cut from the center toward the edge. When you are 3 inches from the edge (or seam) of the material, reverse the cut so that you are cutting into the burlap.

A razor knife is a good tool to use when cutting burlap paper. You should cut from the center toward the outside seams. When you get about 3 inches from the edge of the seam (as mentioned above), reverse the knife and cut back into the material. The razor knife must be sharp; we recommend that you change blades after every 4 rolls of burlap you trim. At inside corners, where the material is overlapped, make sure that the overlapped edge fits tightly against the adjoining wall. If this edge is not tight, the burlap will pop off the wall when the adhesive dries.

Printed burlap looks good, but it does not have the texture of the authentic wallcovering. You have to be especially careful with this product. Lay out the strips so the shading in the texture matches. Vinylized burlap can be a problem since the edges or seams tend to lift. We recommend that you apply paste to the wall at the seam area. Let the adhesive almost dry before you apply the strip. The wet adhesive on the strip will reactivate the paste on the wall, and you should get a good bond at the edges.

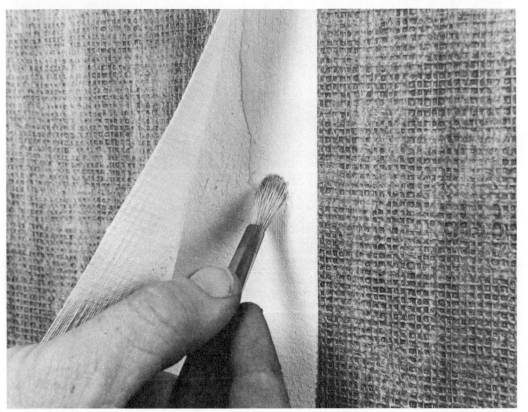

If the printed burlap curls in isolated areas, lift the paper and apply more adhesive to the wall. Then stick the material back down. Although it is not absolutely necessary, we recommend that you cover the walls with lining paper before you hang any type of burlap. Both printed burlap and authentic burlap may shrink. It usually shrinks lengthwise rather than across the paper. Therefore, cut the strips about 5 inches longer than the wall area.

Roll the seams of printed and vinylized burlap lightly. As soon as the paper is in position, wipe away excess adhesive on the face of the paper. Do this after you hang two or three strips. Smooth the paper with a smoothing brush. Work from the center of the strip toward the outer edges, removing air bubbles and wrinkles.

Contact wallcoverings

Contact papers have a peel-and-stick backing. Prepare the walls as you would prepare them for most flexible wallcoverings. However, contact paper is generally used to accent a room rather than to cover all the walls and the ceiling. After you have prepared the walls, drop a plumb bob and snap the chalk line to find a straight edge. Peel about 12 inches of the paper backing, and stick the paper to the wall at the plumb line.

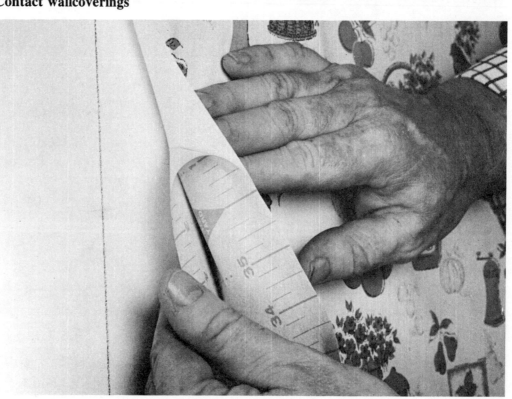

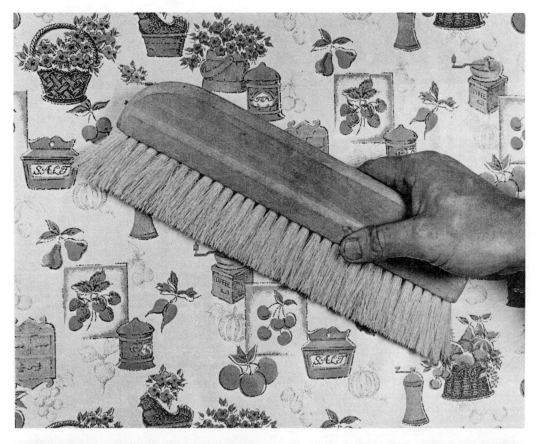

Smooth the contact paper with a regular smoothing brush or a damp sponge. Work from the center of the paper toward the outer edges. If there are large wrinkles in the paper, lift it off the wall and try again. After the first 12 inches of paper are on the wall and it is smooth, remove another 12 inches of the backing and continue the process.

Small bubbles in contact paper may be punctured with a pin. The pin prick releases trapped air behind the paper, and you may press the bubble down on the wall. However, try to work out bubbles and wrinkles with a smoothing brush or a sponge. If you can do this, the paper will look neater. Trim the paper with scissors or a razor knife—as you would trim vinyl or paper wallcoverings.

Specialty Wallcovering Materials

Materials to cover the walls in your home or apartment are not confined to paneling and flexible wallcoverings. You have a wide range of specialty materials from which to choose. These materials can fit a specific design you have in mind, create a mood within the room, or change the appearance of the room.

All of the specialty products are installed in approximately the same way. In this chapter, you will find out how to install the most popular specialty wallcoverings: ceramic tile, cork tile, mirror tile, and simulated brick and stone.

Specialty wallcoverings usually are sold in a package: so many square feet of material to a carton or package. To purchase these materials, you will have to know the area of the wall you want to cover. You will find estimating charts for this in the chapter *How To Estimate Wallcovering Needs*.

Almost without exception, specialty wallcoverings are easy to install. In our opinion, cork tile, mirror tile, and simulated brick and stone are easier to put up than wall paneling and flexible wallcoverings.

The wall surface has to be in top condition before the specialty materials can be applied. Holes in gypsum wallboard and lath and plaster have to be repaired; the patches have to be smooth. Also, peeling paint must be removed from the walls. You can install almost any specialty wallcovering over wallpaper if the wallpaper is tight on the wall. If not, you will have to remove the wallpaper. These preparation procedures are explained elsewhere in the book.

With the exception of ceramic tile, most of the specialty wallcoverings you find in building material outlets, home center stores, hardware stores, and general merchandise centers are designed for accent walls creating a mood.

For example, you will probably not want to cover an entire room—walls and ceiling—with cork, mirrors, or fiber glass brick. This is to your advantage; it is easier to cover a small area than a large one. It is also cheaper.

When working with specialty wallcoverings, keep in mind that colors and textures can completely change the proportions of a room. You must plan the type of room that you would like to have.

Light or pale colors in a room will make it appear larger. Dark colors make the room appear smaller. Contrasting colors are recommended for accents. If there is a glossy surface in the room—or if you are thinking about applying a material with a glossy surface—this surface will appear larger because of the light reflection.

Also, a specialty pattern can change the mood in the room. For example, a material with a vertical pattern will make the wall seem higher than it actually is. A horizontal pattern will make the room look narrower than it is. Horizontal patterns can also make a room look wider than it is. The furnishings in the room play a role too. If you have traditional furniture, it may look best in a square room with a high ceiling. Modern furniture fits well in medium-size rooms with low ceilings. When you are shopping for wallcovering materials, consider the type of furnishings that you will use in the room.

You may want to consider paint as an accent when you choose a wallcovering material.

How to install ceramic tile

There are three different types of tile; the most common is ceramic tile. The other types are plastic tile and metal tile. In this section we show you how to install ceramic tile. The same methods apply to the other types of tile, except that you must use a hacksaw and tinsnips to cut and shape plastic and metal tile.

To install wall tile, find the lowest point in the room. Measure from the floor of each wall to the ceiling. The longest measurement from the floor to the ceiling will be the lowest point.

The walls must be properly prepared. You do not have to worry about hairline cracks in the plaster or gypsum board; the tiles will cover this imperfection.

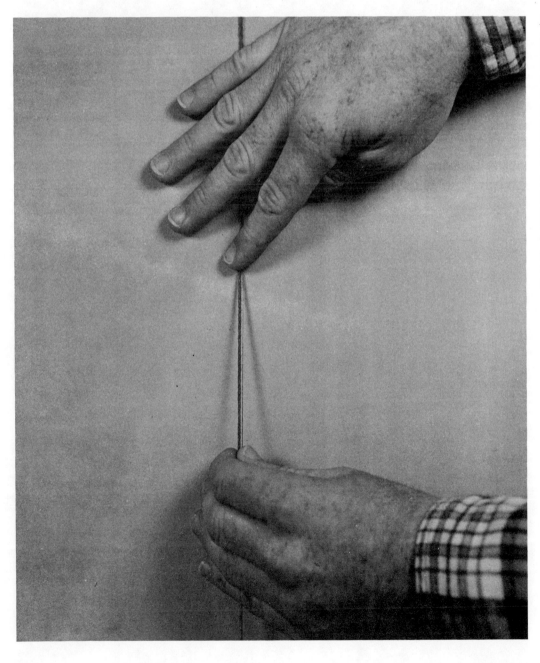

Find the lowest spot in the room, and determine the height you want the tile from this low spot. Mark the spot, adding a half tile for later fitting purposes. Now drop a plumb bob on a chalk line near the lowest point. Holding the plumb bob to keep the line taut, snap the chalk line. The line left on the wall establishes the true vertical, or plumb, and it will serve as a guideline for the tiles. Once you establish this vertical, the other tiles should be true (but you continually have to check them with a level).

Using a field tile as a template, mark off the number of rows of tile you will need starting at the lowest point in the room. If there will be a feature strip of tile on the wall, you have to figure this width in the measurement. Also, you should allow for the cap strip. The cap strip is put on the wall last.

With a carpenter's level, mark a horizontal line around the room—or on the wall—at the height you want the tile. Start at the plumb line. Mark the rest of the rows on the wall. The purpose of this is to make sure that all of the tiles will be at the same height on the wall. Go across the wall, using a tile as a template, and mark the lines starting with the vertical (plumb) line. If you find that you come out less than ½-tile width at either corner of the wall, recenter the tile on the vertical center line and re-mark the wall. Then, you will not have to cut a lot of small pieces of tile to fit. If you can't space out the tiles because the wall is not true and plumb, you will have to cut the tile to fit.

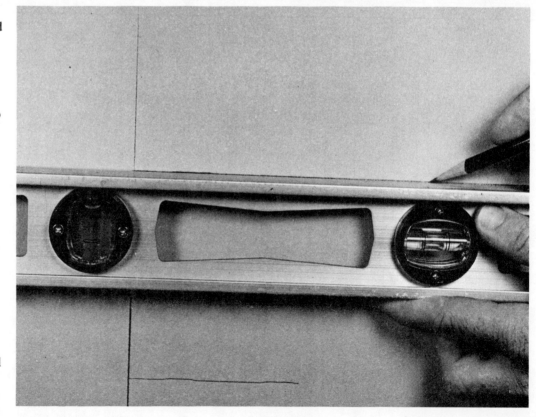

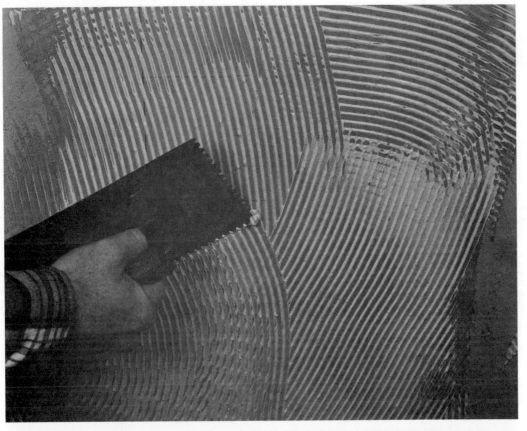

Spread the adhesive on the wall with a notched trowel. Use plenty of tile adhesive. You will be able to see the guidelines underneath the adhesive. Use about one gallon of adhesive for fifty square feet of tile. Check the manufacturer's recommendations on the adhesive container. Start applying the tile where the vertical and horizontal guidelines meet. The best way is to set two vertical rows of tile, then two horizontal rows. Check for level and plumb, and continue the job. The secret is to get the vertical and horizontal rows of tile on perfectly straight; then the rest of the job will follow easily.

To go around pipes and other obstructions, you can nibble away the tile with pliers or regular tile nippers. Take small bits out of the tile; don't try to knock off a big chunk of tile at one time. If the tile breaks, don't try to patch it to the wall. Pick up a new tile and try again.

To break ceramic tile evenly, score the face of the tile with a glass cutter. Then lay the score mark over a box or a casing nail, as shown. Snap the tile with your fingers. The tile will break evenly. The rough edges produced by the cut usually won't show because the tile grout will cover them. However, if this is a problem, smooth the edges of the tile by rubbing them on a concrete block or a brick.

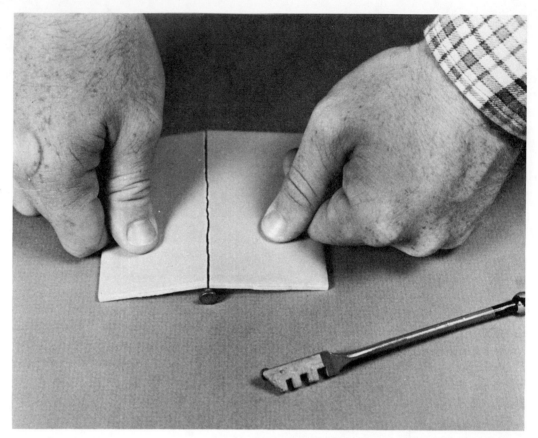

Around obstructions, such as wall switches and outlets, you will have to mark the tile to fit. Use a grease pencil for this, and make the measurements as accurate as you can. You can usually nibble out the tile to fit the obstruction with pliers or nippers. You don't have to be extremely accurate with the pliers since the switch plates will cover the cut.

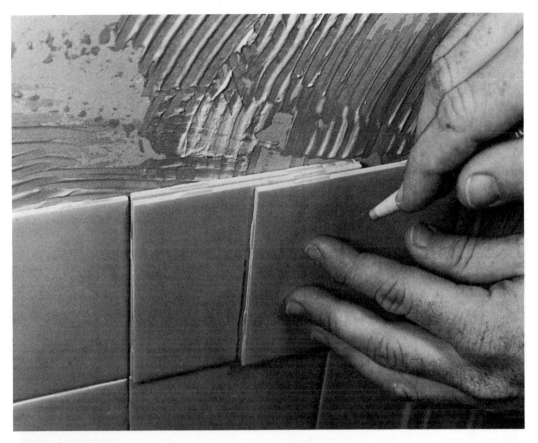

To cut a tile to fit a gap, place a full tile over the last tile you installed. Then put another tile over the gap so that it overlaps the full tile, as shown. Now mark the full tile underneath, using the edge of the top tile as a guide. This will give you an accurate measurement and a cutting point. Score the face of the tile with a glass cutter and snap the tile over a nail. The piece that is left will fit the gap between the last wall tile and the corner.

Clean the tiles with commercial tile cleaner and a sponge when all of the tile is in place and the cap strips are in position. If you can, let the adhesive under the tile dry for a couple of days before you grout the joints. This will protect the adhesive from any moisture from the grout. Then, fill the joints with tile grout. The grout should be the consistency of whipped cream. Press it into the joints with a putty knife, a scraper, or a squeegee. Make sure the joints are completely full of grout, since the grout tends to shrink as it dries.

Use your finger to smooth the grout after it has been applied. When you apply the grout, you should also wet the joints of the tile. This prevents the wall surface from absorbing a lot of moisture from the grouting compound.

After you apply the grout, use a little tile cleaner to remove any excess adhesive and grout from the tile face. If you can, keep the grout lines moist for four or five days. Use plenty of water for this. This keeps the grout from shrinking in the joints and gives you a smoother job. You can also buy a ceramic tile sealer which will help protect the joints; and we recommend that you use it. Make sure the grout is dry before you apply the sealer.

Cork tile and mirror tile

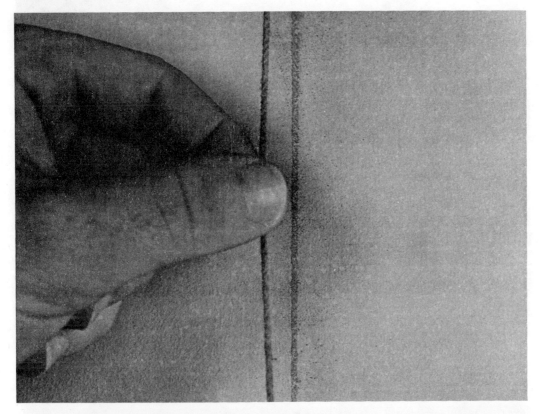

When you install cork tile and mirror tile, snap a plumb line so that the material will be straight on the wall. You should also use a level to make sure the material is horizontally level. The walls have to be level and clean. If they are not level, put up furring strips and cover the walls with tempered hardboard or gypsum wallboard. The tempered hardboard is used more often with mirror tile than with cork tile. Cork tile will conform to uneven walls unless they are extremely uneven. However, the material is brittle, so you have to be very careful when applying cork to the wall—or ceiling.

Most cork tile has a peel-and-stick backing. However, some cork tile requires adhesive. Before you install the peel-and-stick tile, make sure the walls are clean and the cracks are patched. Then snap a level horizontal line halfway from the floor to the ceiling. This will be a working point. We also suggest that you snap a vertical line. Begin to install the tile at the point where the lines intersect. We also recommend that you use a tile as a template and mark off the courses of tiles along the horizontal and vertical lines. If you come out less than ½-tile width at either corner of the wall, recenter the tile on the vertical center line and re-mark the wall.

Cut cork tile on the back side of the tile. Use a carpenter's square or a combination square. A razor knife will cut the tile best, but the tile will crumble slightly as you cut it. The crumbling can't be avoided. However, change the razor blade in the knife often so that you will get a clean cut.

Mark for cuts around electrical switches and outlets with a wax pencil. If you can, try to butt one edge of a tile against the switch, outlet, or other obstruction. Then cut the hole for the electrical switch in the adjoining tile. This is easier than trying to piece and fit two tiles.

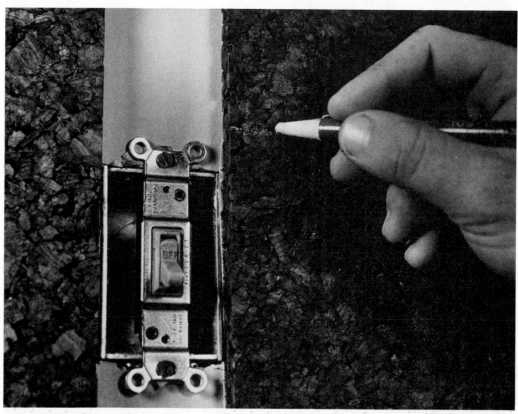

The finished job around an electrical switch or outlet should look like this. To make the switch or outlet flush with the cork tile, you will probably need to inset some tiny wooden shims behind the "ears" of the electrical unit—where the unit is fastened (screwed) to the junction box.

Cork tile often crumbles on the edges. The gaps may be filled by applying cork tile pieces to the voids, using cork tile adhesive to stick the pieces into position, as shown.

If you use adhesive to apply cork tile, apply the adhesive with a notched trowel. Do about a 2-foot wide area at one time; then set the tile in this area. The adhesive dries fairly fast; you do not want to cover more surface with adhesive than you can tile in 10 minutes.

Some cork edges may be exposed. If so, you should butt a piece of molding against the edge of the tiles. This will help keep the tiles from crumbling. Use finishing nails to fasten the molding to the wall, or you can use builder's panel adhesive. Adhesive works best when you can't nail into a stud or joist framing member.

How to install mirror tile

Prepare the walls first. If the mirror squares have a pattern, lay out the squares on the floor and match the patterns. Drop a plumb line and establish the horizontal level. Using one mirror square as a template, go across and down the wall and lay out the tiles—just like ceramic tile and cork tile. Mirror tiles usually come with adhesive pads, which you peel and stick on the wall (as shown). The first tile should be fastened to the wall slightly left of the vertical plumb line. Or, put the tile in position on the marked rows of mirror tiles. Use as many full tiles as possible so you don't have to cut and fit pieces.

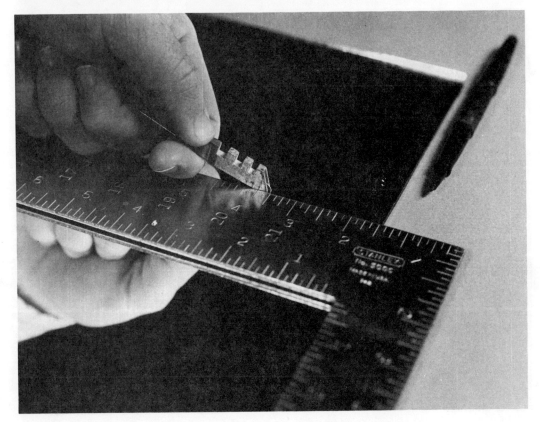

Cut mirror tile with a glass cutter. Use a carpenter's square to get a perfect line. Apply plenty of pressure to the glass cutter, and make just one swipe along the straightedge. This seems to work better than going back and forth over the same cut with the glass cutter. If you have a lot of tiles to cut, change glass cutters frequently. The little cutting wheels become dull fast, and the cost of a new cutter is not prohibitive.

Snap the mirror tile over a dowel rod. The tile should break perfectly over the line scored by the glass cutter. You don't need a lot of pressure to break the tile; just use your thumbs.

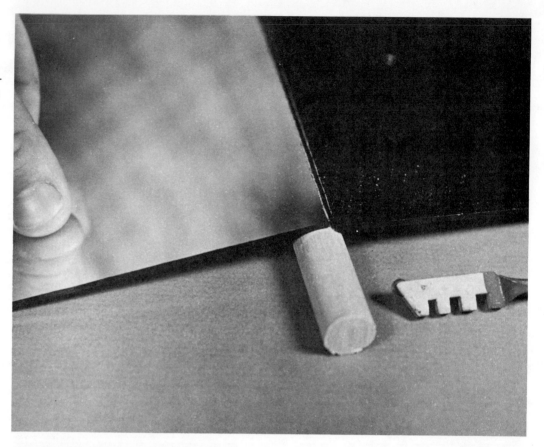

Mirror tile is difficult to fit around electrical outlets, because you have to score and break the glass. You do this by inserting a narrow piece of tile and cutting it lengthwise and crosswise to fit. The joints of the narrow piece at this junction will not be objectionable. It is almost impossible to notch a piece of mirror tile to fit around an obstruction.

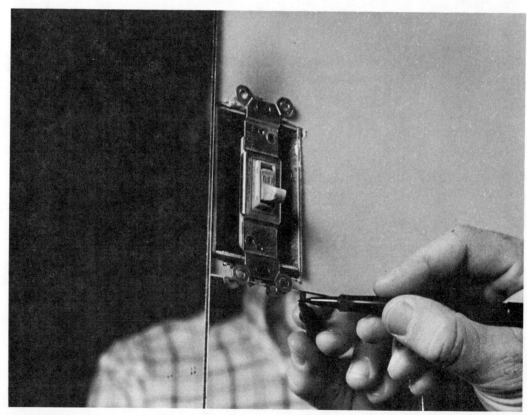

How to install simulated brick and stone

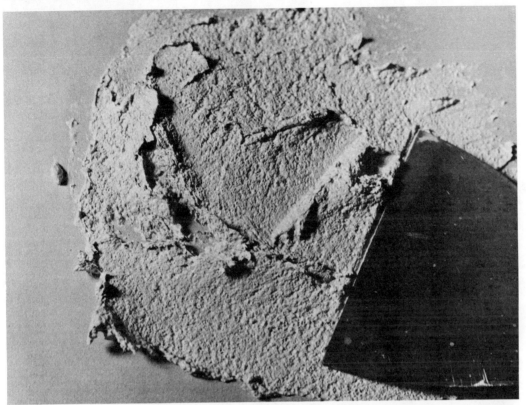

You can buy simulated brick and stone in individual units or sheets. Both types are explained here. Prepare the walls. Individual units of simulated brick and stone should be applied as you would apply ceramic tile. You will have to establish a vertical plumb line and a horizontal line. From this point, mark off the individual units, leaving about 1/2 inch between the joints for a mortar joint. Apply the special adhesive to the wall with a wall scraper or a putty knife. Use plenty of adhesive, since it doubles as the mortar in the joints. But apply adhesive to one small area at a time so that you can follow the guidelines.

Put a level on the first row of bricks. Space them properly—about ½ inch between the joints or according to the manufacturer's recommendations on the carton. You can stack the bricks— one on top of another—or set the bricks in a random pattern. In our opinion, the random pattern looks best in a red or an earth tone color. The white brick looks better in a stacked pattern. Press the bricks firmly into the adhesive.

The adhesive should conform to the wall, but it may be somewhat uneven. If so, we recommend that you use a tuck-pointing trowel to smooth the adhesive. You may also cut an ice cream stick square on one end and use it to smooth the adhesive. To lay out the job, find the lowest point in the room (as explained for ceramic tile). Draw a vertical line at this point, and mark off the bricks for spacing—as you would apply ceramic tile. However, you should leave space for the mortar line. Inside corners should have about a ⅜-inch space on each second row of bricks so that the brick will match. For example, rows 2, 4, 6, and 8 will have the brick against the corner. The adjoining row will have a ⅜-inch space on the even rows. The even number of rows will be flush. You can leave the top row of bricks plain, or you can nail on a piece of molding at the top row. When setting the bricks, wipe off any adhesive on the face of them. You should also check the manufacturer's recommendations on where to install the bricks. Some bricks are not suitable for use in showers. Manufacturers usually recommend that you install asbestos board at the back side of a kitchen range before the bricks are installed.

Fiber glass brick and stone panels

Fiber glass brick and stone panels are made of stone. The stone has been crushed and embedded in a fiber glass mat. If the wall is fairly smooth and even, the panels may be installed over furring strips or applied directly to the wall (nailed to the studs). You should preplan the wall, spacing out the individual units. The units should be plumb and horizontally level. This fiber glass paneling may be used outside.

The fiber glass panels dovetail together. Nail holes are provided in the "mortar" joints. You can buy the panels with the "mortar" in them. Keep a level on the panels as you fasten them to the wall with gypsum board nails or box nails. The same layout procedures apply to the panels that apply to ceramic tile. You do not have to fill hairline cracks in gypsum board walls or lath-and-plaster walls. If you have a large break in the wall that the panel will not cover, the break will have to be repaired.

Grout or mortar is applied to the joints with a caulking gun, or you can buy the panels already "grouted." Cut the nozzle of the grout cartridge wide enough so that you may fill the joints evenly. Operate the caulking gun smoothly and evenly so that you don't overfill the joints.

You can smooth the grout with a tuck-pointing tool, or you can use an ice cream stick that has been cut to fit the width of the "mortar" joints. After the panels have been grouted, they look authentic. Simulated stone also comes in individual and panel units. It is applied the same way as the brick.

Cover It With Paint

Paint is a wallcovering like wallpaper, paneling, and tile. However, paint is probably the easiest wallcovering to apply, and it is fairly inexpensive. You will pay about $8 to $13 per gallon for quality paint; a gallon of paint will cover from 300 to 500 square feet—depending on the surface to be covered.

There are three basic ingredients in paint:
1. The pigment gives the paint its color and body.
2. A vehicle, such as oil or water, suspends the pigment.
3. A thinner gives the pigment and the vehicle the proper consistency.

Interior paints include solvent-thinned paints and water-thinned paints.

Solvent-thinned paints are usually thinned with mineral spirits. They include modified-alkyd and resin-based enamels. Alkyd enamel is also solvent-thinned.

Water-thinned paints are usually thinned with latex particles emulsified in water. You will be involved with three types: rubber, PVA or vinyl, and acrylic. You can also buy thixotropic (dripless paint), epoxy, urethane, and polyurethane paints. All of these materials are thinned with water.

Interior paints are varied and may be confusing when you shop for them. Here's a rundown on interior paints that may help you make a better selection:

Use any type of interior paint for walls. If the walls are made of lath and plaster, make sure the plaster has aged for at least 3 months before you apply the paint. First, you should seal the surface with a flat, oil-based paint, but do not use an oil-based paint in the kitchen or bathroom. In these rooms, use instead an enamel, a rubber-based paint, or an emulsion paint.

If your home has walls made of gypsum wallboard, you may paint this surface with any quality paint that you would use on walls made of lath and plaster.

We recommend a rubber- or a latex-based paint for your walls, since the lap marks from the brush or roller do not show. Tools may be easily cleaned with water.

Ceilings are light-reflecting surfaces, and they should be painted with a flat paint. Use a semigloss paint for kitchen and bathroom ceilings; it is easy to wash. If the ceiling has not been painted before, we recommend that you give it a primer coat of paint before you put on the top coat.

For woodwork and trim, you can use a semigloss, an enamel, or a flat oil-based paint.

When changing from a dark to a light-colored paint, you will need to put on at least two coats. Also, when using an enamel or a semigloss paint, apply an undercoat first.

When you want a transparent paint—so that you can see the wood grain beneath the finish—buy an interior varnish. When the finish dries, coat it with a good paste wax and buff. If the wood is open-grained, such as oak, you will need a wood filler. Fillers are difficult to use; be sure to follow the manufacturer's recommendations. The recommendations will be printed on the filler container.

Buying a stain is tricky because the samples in the paint showroom may be misleading. Try a sample of the stain on the wood that you will stain—if possible.

You need metal paint for metal surfaces. If you have steel windows, always give the steel a primer coat first; then put on the top coat. Aluminum windows do not need a primer. You can use rubber-based paint, enamel, semigloss, and flat paint on both steel and aluminum windows. However, we recommend an oil-based paint on steel windows because of the rust factor.

Wood paneling will take flat paint, semigloss, emulsion, and rubber-based paint. If the wood is porous, you may have to fill the pores first.

If you want to leave the wood in its natural state, apply shellac or varnish to the surface after you clean it. Then wax the surface after the shellac or varnish dries.

If you want a wood tone, stain the wood. Then brush on two coats of varnish or shellac. Sand lightly between coats with a medium-grit abrasive. Now apply a coat of paste wax to the finish and buff the wax.

Light reflecting qualities of paint

When you buy paint, do not overlook a paint's light-reflecting qualities. A light color reflects light; a dark color absorbs light.

For example, white paint reflects 80 percent of the light that strikes it; ivory, 71 percent; apricot-beige, 66 percent; yellow, 65 percent; light buff, 56 percent; green, 51 percent, medium gray, 43 percent; pale blue, 40 percent; deep rose, 12 percent; and dark green, 8 percent.

Colors can also change the appearance of a room. Warm colors, such as brown or rose, produce a feeling of intimacy. They can make a room look smaller. Cool colors, such as blues and greens, make a room appear larger. Light or bright colors expand a surface. Dark colors soak in light; they make a room appear smaller.

How much paint do you need?

The amount of paint you need for walls and ceilings depends on the surface and how many coats of paint you will give the surface. For example, a new plaster wall will absorb about 20 percent more paint than a wall that has been painted before. A masonry surface is porous and will take about 50 percent more paint.

To estimate your paint needs, measure the length and height of the walls and the length and width of the ceilings. Figure 1 gallon of paint for every 500 square feet of normal surface. If you will use a trim paint, figure 1 gallon of trim paint for every 5 gallons of surface paint. For example, if you are painting just one room you may need 2 gallons of surface paint and 1 quart of trim paint.

Buying paint

There are special paints for metal, paneling, masonry, and gypsum board. Below is information on these surfaces and the correct paint to use.

Plaster walls and ceilings. Use flat, semigloss, or latex paint. If needed, use a sealer or an undercoat.

Gypsum wallboard. Use flat, semigloss, casein, or latex paint. If it is needed, use a sealer or an undercoat.

Kitchen and bathroom walls. Use flat, semigloss, or latex paint.

Wood paneling. Use flat, semigloss, shellac, penetrating wood sealer, or latex paint. You may also wax the surface of the paneling after it has been finished.

Wood trim. Use flat, semigloss, shellac, stain, or latex paint.

Heating ducts. Use flat, semigloss, aluminum, metal primer, or latex paint.

Radiators and pipes. Use flat, semigloss, aluminum, metal primer, or latex paint.

Old masonry. Use flat, semigloss, casein, aluminum, or latex paint. If needed, use a sealer or an undercoat.

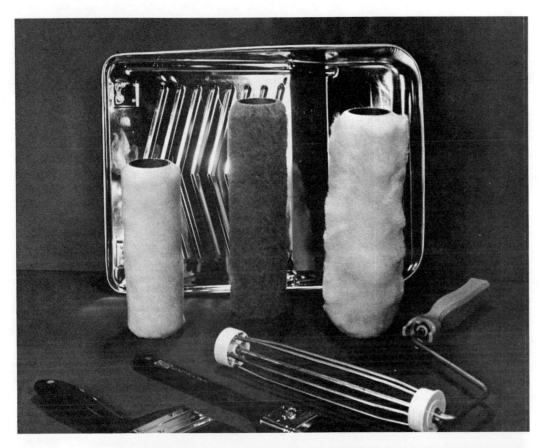

Interior painting equipment includes a roller tray, roller frame, roller covers, a 4-inch wide paintbrush, and an angled sash brush for windows and trim. This equipment costs about $25. If you will be painting ceilings, it is handy to have an extension handle for the roller frame. Also, for most paint jobs, you will need plastic drop cloths, masking tape and a short stepladder. This will add about $10 to the basic cost of your equipment.

Roller covers are made in a variety of nap lengths. You may also choose from several types of covers: Dynel-nylon for use with water emulsion paint; lamb's wool for oil-based paint only; mohair for enamel, varnish, lacquer, and semigloss paint. For rough surfaces such as masonry, you should buy a long-napped roller cover. The short-napped covers are best for use on smooth surfaces. We recommend that you buy a roller frame with a wire frame rather than one of solid metal. If you are using water-based paints, the roller cover should have a plastic base rather than an oiled cardboard base.

Roller cover packages usually provide you with information about the type of roller, what the cover may be used for, size, and cleaning instructions. If the package does not have this information, be sure to ask a sales person in the store to explain how to use the roller cover that you want. Save the polyfilm cover that the roller came in, it makes an excellent storage package for the roller.

Prepare the walls and ceiling surface before you paint. Patching cracks and holes is explained in another chapter. Use the same techniques as you would for flexible wallcoverings, although you don't need lining paper with paint. Cover any surface you don't want painted with masking tape and old newspaper. Rollers produce a fine spray of paint that can ruin adjacent surfaces such as paneling.

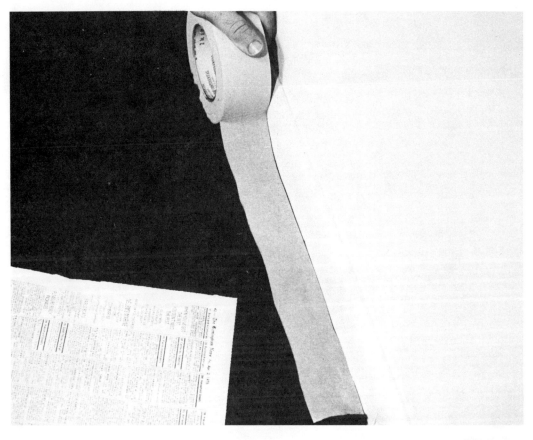

Mask along carpeting. The tape usually holds the nap of the carpeting below the trim board so that you can paint it without painting the carpeting. Also, use masking tape to hold drop cloths tightly against the masking tape that is stuck to the carpeting. The edge of the drop cloth should not gap or bulge at the seam. We recommend 1-inch wide masking tape.

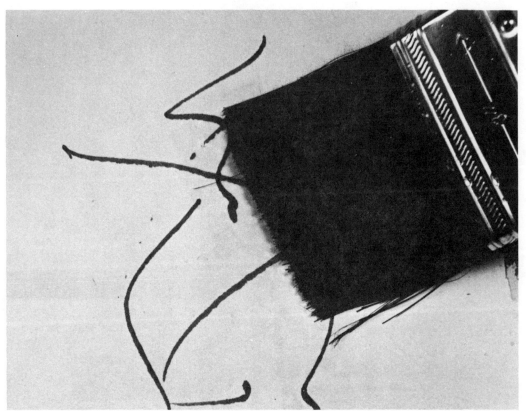

Before you start painting, lightly sand the wall with a fine-grit abrasive on a sanding block. Wipe away any sanding debris with a damp cloth. Let the wall dry about 20 minutes before applying the paint. If there are pen marks, lipstick, or other marks on the wall that might bleed through the new paint, seal them with a light coat of 4-pound cut shellac. The shellac dries quickly.

If you use a brush to paint the walls and ceilings, you don't need a special bucket to hold the paint. However, punch several holes in the rim of the paint container with a nail, as shown. This will permit excess paint to drain back into the container instead of down the side of it. Also, the rim will be easier to "wipe out" with a paintbrush before you put the lid back on the container.

Paint from left to right. On large surfaces such as walls and ceilings, you may reach a larger area by using both hands to control the brush and/or roller. If you use a roller, we recommend that you cut in corners at ceilings and walls with a brush. You can control the brush better for this delicate job. Since most water-based paints are lap-free, you do not have to worry about lap marks when using a brush or roller.

Spread the paint on the wall or ceiling in all directions with a roller. This helps spread the paint more evenly. Use plenty of paint on the roller; don't skimp or the roller will produce tracks on the wall. Keep the roller on the surface, and always work from the dry wall surface to the wet paint.

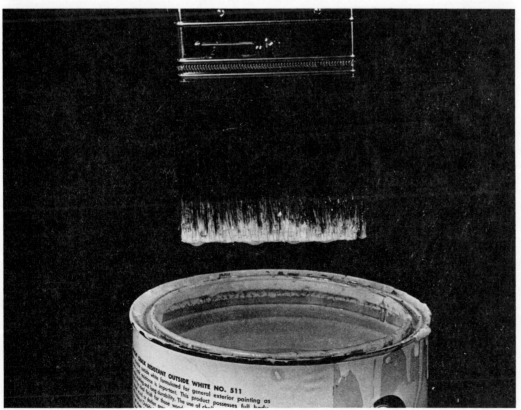

Dip paintbrushes ⅓ the length of the brush's bristles into the paint, as shown. This will keep excess paint out of the heel of the brush and help prevent the paint from running down your arm. Use plenty of paint on the surface, but work with a fairly "dry" brush. The technique is to dip-and-slap the brush, dip the brush in the paint and slap the sides of the brush on the sides of the bucket. If paint runs onto the handle of the brush, wipe this paint off immediately.

To remove loose bristles from a freshly painted surface, daub the tip end of the bristles against the loose bristle. The loose bristle will adhere to the bristles in the brush, and you can pick off the loose bristle. If the brush seems to be losing a lot of bristles, stop painting and wash the brush thoroughly.

Paint roller tracks are caused by the roller skidding on the wall or ceiling surface. If a roller is too dry or has too much paint on the cover, it may skid. Practice will teach you how much paint to apply to the roller. Three complete revolutions of the roller in the tray usually loads the roller cover properly.

To clean a roller cover, remove all excess paint by running the tools over an old newspaper, as shown. Get as much paint as you can out of the roller cover or brush. This technique applies to both oil-based and water-based paints.

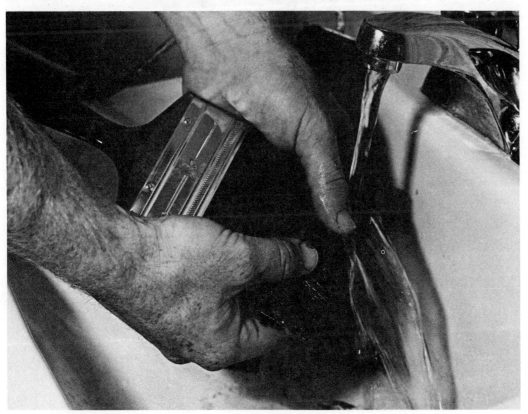

Rinse out excess water-based paint under a faucet, as shown. If you are using an oil-based paint, rinse the brush or roller cover in mineral spirits. Then wash the brush roller with a mild detergent and water. If the paint is water-based, we recommend that you use a mild detergent and scrub the brush or roller cover until the tools are clean.

Wrap the brush or roller cover in aluminum foil or plastic wrap after the bristles or cover are clean. This keeps the bristles in the correct shape until you use the brush again; it keeps dust and dirt off the roller cover nap. When you are painting and want to take time out, you can wrap either a brush or a roller cover in aluminum foil or plastic wrap without cleaning. Make sure the seal is airtight so that the paint won't harden on the bristles or roller cover nap.

Index

Mitering, 30
Moldings and trim, 21, 22
    Cutting, 30, 31
    Estimating, 16

O

Outlets, trimming electrical, 21, 27, 30, 33, 58,
    72, 76, 77, 80

P

Paint, Painting, 85, 86
    Clean-up, 93
    Equipment, 87, 88
    Preparation for, 88, 89
    Technique, 90, 91, 92
Paneling
    Simulated brick and stone, 6, 83, 84
    Wooden, 6, 10, 12
        Estimating, 16
        Installing, 25, 26, 29
        Tools, 13
Paper
    Contact, 19, 66, 67
    Lining, 32, 33, 50, 51
    Wallpaper. *See* Wallpaper
Paste. *See* Adhesives
Preparing walls, 20, 36
    Cracks, 37, 38
    Holes, 39, 49, 41, 42
    Nail pops, 37
    Removing loose wallcovering, 43
    Tools, 14

R

Removing
    Bubbles. *See* Bubbles
    Wallpaper, 43

S

Silk wallcovering, 35
Stain, 86
Stone, simulated. *See* Brick and stone

T

Tile
    Ceramic, 69–74
    Cork, 75–78
    Estimating, 18
    Mirror, 75, 79, 80
    Tools, 13
Tools
    Mitering, 30
    Painting, 87, 88
    Wallcovering, 13–15
    Wall preparation, 36
Trim
    Cutting, 30
    Estimating, 16
Trimming wallpaper, 51, 53, 54, 55

V

Varnish, 10, 86
Vinyl wallcoverings, 33, 34

W

Wainscotting, 7, 11
Wallcoverings, Flexible and rigid. *See* Specific
    types
Wallcovering tools, 13, 14
Wallpaper, 32, 33. *See* Specific types
Wall preparation. *See* Preparing walls
Windows
    Paneling, 22
    Papering, 58